Paris, San Francisco—both beautiful towns, both walking towns. To live in either is to bask in the reflection of the ineluctable.

Réalités

TOULOUSE-LAUTREC.
THE CABARET SINGER ARISTIDE BRUANT.

VULCAN STREET

Stairway Walks

IN SAN FRANCISCO

by Adah Bakalinsky

Drawings by Trudie Douglas

Maps by Bill Chase

LEXIKOS

SAN FRANCISCO

First published in 1984 by
Lexikos
4079 19th Ave.
San Francisco, CA 94132

Edited by Alan Magary
Designed by Q R inc
Production by Carlton Herrick/Q R inc
Text set in Palatino
Printed and bound by Edwards Brothers

Manufactured in the United States of America.

Library of Congress Cataloging in Publication Data

Bakalinsky, Adah.
   Stairway walks in San Francisco.

   1. San Francisco (Calif.)—Description—Tours.
2. Walking—California—San Francisco—Guide-books.
3. Stairs—California—San Francisco—Guide-books.
I. Title.
F869.S33B35 1984   917.94'610453   82-81462
ISBN 0-938530-10-0

   86 87 5 4 3 2

This book is dedicated to Max, who can make a walk to the grocery store an adventure, to our parents, Morris and Helen Packerman and Joseph and Selma Bakalinsky, to our children, Eric, Polly, Mimi, and Alan—and to our grandsons, Noah and Kieran, all good walkers.

1 INCH TO 1.2 MILES

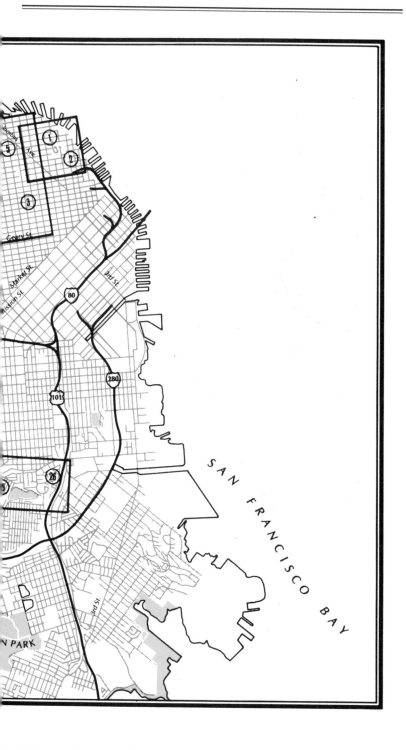

CONTENTS

ILLUSTRATIONS

MAPS

PREFACE

San Francisco is a "walking city." Built upon forty-two hills, it is surrounded by the Bay on the east, the Pacific on the west, a peninsula on the south, and on the north, the Golden Gate. Within those confines, variety is constant. Light and water combine to produce striking effects on bridges and buildings. The Bank of America at 555 California Street is a scintillating pattern of reflections. San Francisco's weather produces subtle color changes in the sky. Throughout the day this provides a seductive backdrop for signs, unfinished structures, and hills.

The hills accelerate changes in perspective as one walks around corners or circles the ridges. Landmarks recede and suddenly emerge in a landscape abounding in inclines and angled streets. The Mount Sutro television tower viewed from the mid-Sunset district is a beautiful sky sculpture; from the Sutro area, it looks like a ship in space. From Ashbury Heights, it looks pedestrian. It appears large and within touching distance from the outer Sunset district; walk two blocks toward it, and it is small and oh so far away.

The streets of San Francisco range from flat, such as Irving, to almost vertical like sections of Duboce and Filbert. In fact, the City Fathers and developers found grading the streets a primary obstacle in turning San Francisco from a tent town into a city of timbered houses. Some of the hills were completely demolished in the process; others were cut into without much planning. When the task seemed insurmountable, the "street" ended.

How does one maneuver from one street level to another when there are so many hills? Via stairways, of course! There are more than 350 stairways—crooked, straight, short, long, concrete, wooden, balustraded, or unadorned. Paved streets often follow the contours of hills, but the stairways allow direct vertical access from one street to another. They are a surprise wherever one finds them and they are one of the least celebrated aspects of San Francisco.

Many of the stairways are not easily identified. In some cases, the Structural Engineer's Office may have a name listed but no sign posted. In other cases, the stairway is not officially listed because it is privately maintained. I have named these stairways by referring to the closest cross street.

The twenty-six walks in this book vary in length and elevation. They are designed for the curious walker—but there are some that billy goats and St. Bernards would love. Each walk takes two to three hours if you enjoy all the sights, scents, and sounds along the way.

Pacific Heights, Russian Hill, and other well-known areas are included, but I have focused more attention on neighborhoods that are not usually featured in guidebooks and not well-known to residents of other San Francisco neighborhoods.

The starting points of every walk can be reached by car or by public transportation (call 673-MUNI for information).

Some of the walks are quite strenuous, although I feel the stupendous views and delightful discoveries justify the strain. Buses are available at several points of most walks, and alternate routes are occasionally suggested for the faint of breath or footstep.

I have found it worthwhile to carry binoculars because the views throughout add to the enjoyment of the walks. You might even bring a compass to help correlate the descriptions of the terrain with the views around you.

Five impressions became more distinct as I searched for stairways in San Francisco.

One: San Francisco is very woodsy. I venture an educated guess that the proportion of open space to built-up space is about one to three.

Two: San Francisco has thousands of views, from panoramic to miniature. Some of the most notable ones, ones that visitors should see but usually don't, are in areas secluded by hilly, craggy terrain. An untapped source of changing views is *between* the houses as one walks by.

Three: Our street system is undisciplined. Only the most hardy, fearless citizen can personally know all the obscure streets and alleys. Then one must recheck street names; they have a way of doubling back upon themselves, halving and disappearing altogether. In addition, once a street is legally named it continues to be listed on maps even though it may be blocked off or terminated.

Four: Both commercial and official maps are inaccurate. I used a collection of them for checking and counter-checking because none seemed to walk the way they looked. After several rewalkings and frustrating reroutings, I took Gene Smith out to integrate the walked and the written. Her maps were the models for Bill Chase's finished maps.

Five: The city parts fit together. The hills form a scaffold for the disparate jutting, circular and rectangular areas. Streets connect one neighborhood to another.

After years of walking in San Francisco, enjoying the ambience, and feeling extremely lucky that I live here, my most rewarding surprise was realizing that I felt the geography of San Francisco. I knew it!

The shape of San Francisco is indelibly imprinted in my bones and on my psyche. I used its image as my framework in designing the stairway walks, keeping in mind the corridor streets that allow us to walk the width and length of the city.

Happy heeling, frisky footing, and merry walking.

Acknowledgements. What began as child's play—how many stairways can we find, how many steps can we leap over and how fast can we ascend them—gradually became an introduction to city geography and history. When we became more disciplined, stairway play became a book project. The idea of a book came from Judith Lynch, who senses ideas before people find words for them. She was coordinator of City Guides, a volunteer group of goodwill ambassadors who give free historical and architectural walks in San Francisco under the sponsorship of Friends of the Public Library.

Many City Guides volunteered their time and services toward the completion of this book: Sue Haas, Daniel Warner, Alice Henry, Janet Tom, Barbara Kerrigan, Anne Thomas, Linda Frieze, Wendy Blakeman, and Tom Filcich. Gladys Hansen, City Archivist, patiently answered questions and found pertinent reference materials for me. Artist and City Guide Trudie Douglas was an inspiration from the beginning of the project. Her superb artistry, craftsmanship, and meticulous concern for details helped us maintain a high standard. Gene Smith, working quietly, capably, and with conviction and humor, made pattern and order visible on the original maps from our walking notes and her on-site observations.

Additional non-guide friends who helped type away chaos from lists are Willy Werby, Eytha Baschen, and Eric Bakalinsky. Friends who walked the routes checking text and maps for clarity and accuracy are Joan and Fred Groves, Noah Walker, Mimi Melody, Bonnie Trach, Robert and Lillian Burt, Robert and Adele Donn, Elizabeth Lembke, Mildred Hamilton, James Milestone, and James Delgado. Additional thanks to Bea Hendon, Andy Husari, Sylvia Graff, Lyda Dykas, Margann Dowd, Bob Szarnick, the kind people along Vulcan and Pemberton stairways, Ilse Dickmann, John Coady, Phil Wong of the Structural Engineers Office for help in understanding official data, and Ray Rossin and Jeanne Fisher for sundry tasks.

A very special thanks to Edna Williams who inspired me to continue exploring after she introduced me to the hills of San Francisco, and to my editor, Alan Magary, who encouraged me to write in my own style.

Adah Bakalinsky

MAP A

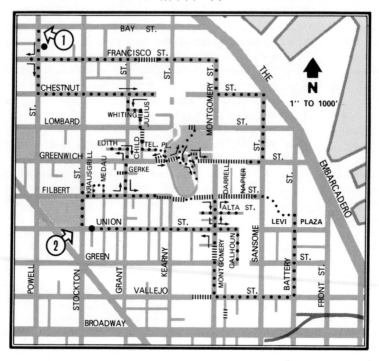

1 □ Hills and Fills
2 □ Mazes and Labyrinths

MAP KEY

Begin	End	Stair	Path	Street

Hills and Fills

Lower Telegraph Hill, where we begin, borders the northern waterfront and Fisherman's Wharf with its colorful banners, outdoor crab pots, and never-ending procession of people.

Here in its early days, San Francisco had its breweries, forges, and slaughterhouses; its wine, meat, and produce wholesalers worked farther along toward Sansome Street.

Being near the waterfront and the railroad spur made this area seem the pulsing heart of the city—though the real heart lay in the financial district where the money was.

In the 1960s, this place was dynamic. Around the base of Telegraph Hill were stores selling whatever could be imported, hotels and hostelries for sailors and travelers, and shanty towns the Australian contingent called Sydneytown and the South Americans called Little Chile. It's not difficult to imagine the international fracases, the multitude of murders, and the ensuing backlash from the vigilantes.

The 1906 earthquake leveled everything in this quarter except the Ferry Building, which at that time was one of the tallest buildings in San Francisco. The area was soon rebuilt, and many of the businesses continued as before, up to the present day. The remaining warehouses comprise an historic district.

Throughout this walk, we can almost hear era after era dissolving into its successor.

■ We begin at the intersection of Powell and Bay, walk south on Powell, and turn right on Francisco for a moment to see the large post-earthquake brick structure on the south side of the street. Until 1980, this was the Bauer-Schweitzer Malting Company, the last barrel malting factory west of the Mississippi. Their high quality malt was sold to small American breweries, such as Anchor, and exported to Japan. When it became economically infeasible to continue operations, the building was sold and is currently being renovated for condomimiums. Because of its landmark status, the exterior will be unchanged, and some of the malting equipment will be displayed in the public areas.

□ We return to Powell, walk south, then left on Chestnut.

□ Two blocks down, at the intersection of Grant Avenue and Chestnut, we have a long view of Marin toward the north and west. Before us, we see the boats anchored at Fisherman's Wharf, Piers 33 and 35, and perhaps a container ship moving slowly into port. Farther in the distance is Pier 39, renovated in the 1970s for shops and restaurants; north of it is Angel Island State Park, part of the Golden Gate National Recreation Area.

☐ No. 298 Chestnut is a Mediterranean-type home built in 1929, its tile roof, marble entry, and ceramic Della Robbia plaque visible through iron gates. The north side of Chestnut here is now officially designated as Open Space; this means that all plantings—a jade plant in bloom, a cotoneaster, a mirror plant, and junipers—will remain as they are.

☐ We've come to a dead end and must backtrack past the extensive and beautifully landscaped gardens of 241-45 Chestnut to Grant Avenue.

☐ At Grant Avenue, we turn left and go south, turning left again at Whiting. A half-block down, walk up the nine steps of Julius Street, an alley at the end of Whiting. Almost directly across from us are the 29 steps of Child Street taking us to Telegraph Place. Here we turn left and walk to the left of the chain link, to get to Telegraph Hill Boulevard, where we turn right.

☐ Next to No. 210 are steps to the Greenwich Street cul-de-sac. We walk up the fifty cement Greenwich steps on the south side of the street to Telegraph Hill Boulevard. We cross the road to the beautiful Greenwich stone steps (with hand rail) and walk up.

☐ We have arrived at the pedestrian road behind Coit Tower, one of the universally recognized symbols of the city, built in 1935 in honor of the San Francisco Fire Department. It rises 179 feet from the crest of Telegraph Hill, itself 284 feet high.

☐ Near Telegraph Place we sit a moment on a long concrete bench, our backs to the rocks, to enjoy the view. A medallion of Marconi, inventor of the telegraph, is at the center of the tastefully designed planting area nearby.

■ As we walk back toward Coit Tower, we are aware of the recurring wavy shapes of the macadam beneath our feet, like so many loaves of bread, all formed by the constant erosion caused by the tree roots.

☐ We turn right on the redwood bark path, and sit down on the bench for a sparkling view of the Ferry Building and its famous clock dating from 1895.

☐ Directly in front of us is the Transamerica Pyramid; the tall building of dark carnelian granite is the Bank of America. The graduated towers to the right of it are part of Embarcadero Center, a well-designed complex on the site of the old wholesale produce market. Because Embarcadero Center is on redevelopment land, and the developer had to spend one percent of the total cost of the buildings on art works. The sculpture and woven hangings are very impressive.

☐ As we walk along the left side of Coit Tower, we can look inside and see WPA murals from the 1930s. Intermittent vandalism makes it necessary at times to close the mural rooms to visitors, but for the elevator ride to the top floor, Coit Tower is always open to the public in

GREENWICH STREET

the daytime. The parking lot has coin telescopes that bring a closeup view of the east side of the Bay.

☐ We walk down the stairs at the front of the Tower and proceed on the footpath to the right until we come to the continuation of the Greenwich Street stairs, this section is brick. Here the stairway does not continue in a straight line, but meanders, and there is room on each side for wide, terraced private gardens, behind which the rooftops peek out. The lane running at right angles from No. 356 Greenwich has no name. It connects with the Filbert steps further to the south (Walk 2).

■ The first landing of these 147 stairs leads down to Montgomery's cul-de-sac and the famous Julius' Castle restaurant, built in 1923. A beautiful mature fig tree graces the entrance.

☐ Pause to look back up these extremely photogenic stairs, surely among San Francisco's most pleasant. The brick of the lower retaining wall is arranged in a haphazard pattern with protruding stones and a wooden balustrade.

☐ Crossing Montgomery—which is like an opera singer taking a deep breath—we come to the Greenwich sign and descend the 210 concrete steps broken by several landings. There's a cistern for firefighting and, on the left side of the walkway, are trees, gardens, and a bench. The simple board and shingle house at 233 Greenwich has a red door. A beautiful purple Princess tree (*Pleroma*) dominates the garden across from No. 237; plum and magnolia trees complement it in shape and color.

☐ As there are plays within plays, at Nos. 231 and 233 there are additional private stairways within public ones. The hillsides are usually full of nasturtiums and fennel, both edible, and great additions to salads. In season, blackberries are for the picking. The building to the right is part of the Levi Strauss Plaza (Walk 2).

☐ At the foot of the steps to Sansome Street, turn left. To the left is 101 Lombard, a new condominium.

■ The eastern slope of Telegraph Hill, as seen from Sansome and Lombard, was extensively quarried from 1860 to 1914. The material was used as landfill in the Bay, enlarging the warehouse district and forming the Embarcadero seawall and roadway. The Gray Brothers Artificial State and Paving Company quarried many of the city's curbs and sidewalks here. Their embossed concrete insignia is a common sight.

☐ Continuing on Sansome, we reach a handsome brick building at Chestnut Street, formerly a warehouse and now a health center. Turn left on Chestnut. One block up is a three-story brick building angled across the corner of Montgomery and Chestnut. It was built in the late

1800s and reconstructed in 1973. We turn right on Montgomery and left to Francisco.

☐ Along Francisco, there is a practical, permanent wooden stairway beginning in the yard of Wharf Plaza 1 and 2, a HUD-assisted project between Kearny and Grant. Quickly ascending the 79 steps, we're at Grant Avenue. Continue west on Francisco.

☐ According to the sign in front, the little cottage at No. 276 dates from 1863. Delicious aromas surround No. 271, now a cooking school.

☐ We turn right at Powell Street and see a variety of storefronts. What was once a well-known sculptor's studio is now a restaurant, and at No. 2202, the Old Venetian Bakery is now a theater. At the corner is a cable car stop.

☐ And here we are at our beginning—with a choice of all compass points for other inspiring looksees.

☐ The Cost Plus import store nearby on Taylor is a popular place to buy trinkets and inexpensive housewares. Six blocks west, at the foot of Columbus, is The Cannery, an unusual shopping complex; two blocks beyond is Ghirardelli Square, another historic setting for specialty shops (Walk 6 ends in this area).

☐ Listen closely: it's still possible to hear one lively era dissolving into the present.

Mazes and Labyrinths

North Beach and Telegraph Hill are contiguous neighborhoods whose informal boundaries extend from diagonal Columbus Street to the Embarcadero on the Bay front, and from Broadway on the south to Jefferson on the north.

Hundreds of alleys, lanes, and stairways are, for some inhabitants, the only significant paths of everyday travel here. Almost any street has visual interest enough to occupy the senses. The ambience is a distillation of the past—artists and writers and musicians of the twenties, the Beat Generation of the fifties, and the young executives of the late seventies and early eighties.

Recently the predominantly Italian community has modified into a more mixed neighborhood; interspersed among Italian bakeries, delicatessens, and restaurants are Chinese bakeries, delicatessens, and restaurants.

This walk is strenuous, so it has been designed on the Angleworm Principle—it can be cut up into two parts, each of which may regenerate into a separate entity.

You may want to begin in the "lowlands" of Battery Street and walk to the "highlands" of Stockton and Union (very strenuous). Or, you may want the circular walk that ends where we begin. Or, you may want to stay with us as we begin in the highlands and finish among the old warehouses on Sansome, examples of intelligent architecture and planning. Public transportation is available throughout this walk.

■ We begin, at Stockton and Union Streets, by the Italian national church Saint Peter and Paul, which offers a Sunday morning mass in Cantonese. The park across the street is Washington Square, the informal community center for resting, picnics, sunning, contemplation, and sports.

☐ On Stockton, walk north for a block and a half to No. 1736, designed by Bernard Maybeck in 1909 for the Telegraph Hill Neighborhood Association as living quarters for nurses and settlement workers. The brown redwood-shingled exterior—colorful with windowbox geraniums—still retains the inviting quality of the hand crafted style that Maybeck developed in the early 1900s. Plants, patios, and interiors renovated as offices for architects and designers create a bright and pleasant working environment.

☐ The neighboring buildings on Stockton are post-earthquake Edwardian flats: Three- or four-story wood-frame flats with separate entrances; the first story has a flat front and the upper stories have bay windows. The Napoli Grocery Store at No. 1756 has been there for fifty years and is now owned by Chinese.

☐ We retrace our steps half a block to the corner of Filbert and Stockton, where the Liguria Bakery has been in business since 1912. Its specialty is *focaccia,* a soft-dough pizza.

☐ Strolling east on Filbert we have the pick of several alleys to explore. In the maze is Krausgrill Place, but it turns into a U and becomes another alley, Medau Place. Krausgrill has a galvanized iron hitching post and bollards. Medau has so-called Romeo flats: high balconies Romeo would approve of (good examples are Nos. 19 and 29 Medau Place). Romeo flats are an interesting architectural variation scattered throughout the city.

☐ We continue east on Filbert. At Grant Avenue, turn left, walking past the Pardee Alley stairway between Kramer and Gerke. Farther along is Edith Street, a charming offshoot to explore. The flats here are typical of alleys whose narrow width (12 feet is standard) precludes bay windows. No. 21 has window boxes of geraniums, No. 27 has vines on the sides of the house, and No. 35 has decorative arches. A Vitruvian scroll and planters of fragrant green shrubs enliven the doorway of No. 35. From the open gate at 60 Edith, there is an unexpectedly fine view of curvy Lombard Street and the Golden Gate Bridge.

■ We return to Grant, turning right back toward Filbert, where we turn left, going eastward, and walk up the sidewalk stairway on the north side of the street until the new Garfield Elementary School, built in 1979, comes into view.

☐ The building of Garfield School was unique. The school principal and the architects (Esherick, Homsey, Dodge, and Davis) spent two years asking teachers, students, parents, and neighbors how the school should fit into the community. The award-winning building hugs the terrain and the beautifully shaped sidewalk stairway. The exterior is painted in four terracotta colors, blending without blinding. There are 16 classrooms; a greenhouse adjoins the library. With Coit Tower looming above the school, the children have history peering through the windows. Only from indoors is it apparent that the school has four levels. Except for six inner rooms with skylights, every room on the lower levels has a view of the Bay Bridge and the skyscrapers. The fourth level has views of the Golden Gate Bridge and the west. From kindergarten to the fifth grade, Garfield children spend their school days in a beautiful, energizing environment.

☐ We cross Kearny at a cul-de-sac to walk the stairs to Telegraph Hill Boulevard. Acacia, eucalyptus, Monterey cypress, and various shrubs are close at hand, and the hummingbirds are chipping. At the top of the stairs, No. 115 seems to be an 1850s cottage.

FILBERT STREET

☐ The boulevard continues around the left. A parallel footpath connects the Filbert and Greenwich stairways to our north (Walk 1). We proceed down the concrete Filbert stairs alongside azaleas, violets, bamboo, and plum.

■ The upper section of the Filbert stairs is landscaped. Side stairways lead to private dwellings. All of the houses here that date from before the earthquake have been remodeled. No. 300 is a 1940 home with a garden of fruit trees—Satsuma plum, cherry, and Eureka lemon. A tall white tulip tree shares the yard with a plaster-of-paris model of "Creation," sculpted by Ralph Stackpole for the 1939 World's Fair on Treasure Island. It is now protected from the elements by twenty coats of varnish and resin, plus gold leaf.

☐ Across from the stairway is The Shadows restaurant, a fire-red Italianate cottage with shutters bordered by bamboo and rhododendron. In the late 1920s, this building was a grocery store.

☐ We descend to Montgomery Street, narrow at this point and divided; the greenery continues around the high retaining wall and the houses. We stop for a moment in the middle of the street to look at the sgraffito panels on the side of the "moderne" apartment house at 1360 Montgomery. One shows The Worker holding the globe of the world above the Bay Bridge. The bridge towers on the panel are repeated by the actual Bay Bridge towers just beyond it. What extraordinary planning! It trumps *trompe l'oeil* even if it doesn't fool the eye.

☐ We detour from upper Montgomery to the right into Alta, a charming alley, and continue south to Union Street, turning into the Union cul-de-sac. Nos. 291, 291-A, and 287 were built in the 1860s.

☐ A turn right on upper Calhoun gives a giddy sense of tremendous height. No. 9 Calhoun, another home from the 1860s, is supposed to have been spared the 1906 fire by being drenched with wine-soaked rags.

☐ Another U-turn takes us to lower Calhoun and a short stairway to peer over the densely foliated eastern cliff of Telegraph Hill, maintained by a resident of the street.

■ Back up to Montgomery, we turn right into a cul-de-sac on lower Alta Street. No. 33 dates from 1852 and No. 62 sports a mural of ducks.

☐ The best and most complete view of flat, long Treasure Island is from the lower end of Alta. Treasure Island was the site of the 1939 World's Fair and is now United States Navy property. The Navy-Marine Museum is open daily.

☐ A right out of Alta to lower Montgomery, then another right takes us to the descending Filbert Stairway, which begins next to 1360

Montgomery. As the setting of Lauren Bacall's apartment in *Dark Passage*, a 1947 movie made with Humphrey Bogart, this building has been seen by millions of people who have never set foot in San Francisco. The exterior of white concrete is in the shape of a ship, complete with a ship-like upper deck. Etched into the glass over the central entrance are a gazelle, palm trees, and ocean waves.

□ A plaque on the Filbert stairs says: "Filbert Steps, Darrell Place, Napier Lane. In appreciation of Grace Marchant for unselfish, devoted energy in the beautification of Filbert Gardens." The late Grace Marchant moved to the Filbert Steps in 1950, when the area was a dumping ground thirty feet deep. The city gave her permission to burn the dump, and it burned—for three days straight. For decades, she labored on the stairway gardens which were dedicated to her on May 4, 1980; the city contributes water for maintenance.

■ Darrell Place and Napier Lane are "paper streets." They appear as streets on maps and in street guides, but Napier consists only of twelve-foot wooden planks and a wooden stairway—shades of ghost towns left over from Gold Rush days—and Darrell is more like a trail.

□ Fire is always a hazard, and in these areas where there is no room for trucks the Fire Department stores equipment as inconspicuously as possible. Next to the blue fire hydrants on the walkway (blue is the code for connection to a high-pressure system) is a storage box for two small city fire hydrants, and a hose.

□ An undulating walkway planted with rose bushes leads to No. 273 Filbert; the second round upper stories of the flats at No. 267 identify this as a 1930s building. The total effect of the Victorian No. 224—yellow paint, gabled roof, and bougainvillea on the walls and with a princess tree, pyracantha, and iris in the yard—is delightful.

□ The Gothic cottage at No. 228 (1873) was used as a grocery store. Next door, No. 226, a miner's shack from 1863 is being renovated.

□ Concrete forms the lower part of Filbert Stairway, and many of the wild nasturtiums, fennel, and blackberries once profuse along the sides of the hill have been cut down.

■ Once on Sansome Street, the patterned aggregate plaza walk of the new corporate headquarters of Levi Strauss invites us forward. The architects were Hellmuth, Obata & Kassabaum; landscaping by Lawrence Halperin Associates. The complex, of glass and red brick (to blend with neighboring landmarks) with open steel and glass corridors, consists of five buildings extending from Sansome to Battery and the Embarcadero. Shadows and reflections make the whole complex sparkle. Adding to the self-sufficiency of the environment and to

BEADS !!

the amenities for the 3000 employees are a bank, a travel service, a bookstore, a bakery, and restaurants. Outside, there are benches for sunning and lunching to the soothing sounds of a waterfall cascading over sculptured rocks.

☐ Across the plaza is the three-story brick exterior of the old Italian Swiss Colony Wine warehouse, a parade of arches. One of the conditions set down by the Landmarks Commission was that Levi Strauss keep the original exterior of the warehouse and renovate it to earthquake specifications. Through the windows we can see the I-beam earthquake bracing. The original interior contained a well that was useful in halting a roof fire in 1906.

☐ Walking through the courtyard, turn right on Battery. Along here are antique furniture stores and Bus Van, an interesting place to buy supposedly unclaimed objects left in storage. The historic Feather Factory building at 950 Battery used to be a poultry processing plant where feathers were cleaned, sorted, and stuffed into pillows.

☐ We turn right on Vallejo Street. Again we see an excellent view of the east side of Telegraph Hill in all its geologic grandeur in a pattern of earth strata called the Franciscan formation.

☐ An aside: At 202 Green Street, between Sansome and Montgomery, is a plaque dedicated to Philo Farnsworth, who had his laboratory there from 1926 to 1938 when he was perfecting the first television system that worked. He filed over eighty television patents.

☐ We turn right, going northward on Montgomery and walk up the stairway.

☐ At Union we turn left. At No. 487, near Grant Avenue, we pass the oldest bead store in San Francisco, where it is possible to obtain beads of every description.

☐ And here we are at Stockton Street, at our beginning.

MAP B

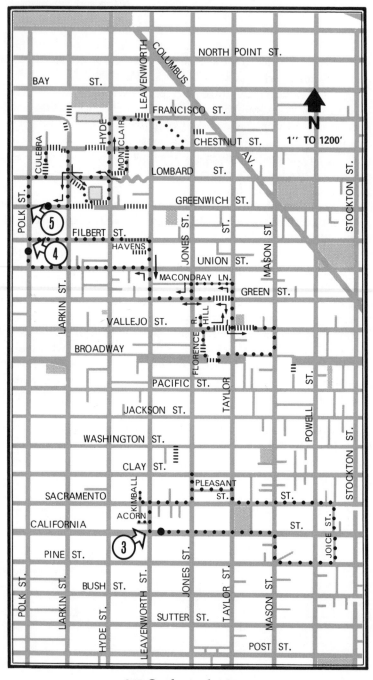

3 □ Castles in the Air
4 □ Speaking of Intangibles
5 □ Architectural Signatures

12

Castles in the Air

Nob Hill, 376 feet above the bay, is wedged in between Pacific Heights to the west, Russian Hill toward the north, and North Beach and Chinatown to the east. Millions of tourists have traversed Nob Hill on the cable cars, gliding both north-south on Powell Street between Market Street and Fisherman's Wharf and east-west on California Street. In 1984, the city will welcome the cars back after an absence of two years during which the system was renovated.

As our bird's-eye view from the top—California Street between Mason and Taylor—comes into focus, we see lines of formidable structures of defense. The inner line of defense (yes, we did feel like Napoleon viewing his fortifications) consists of Hotels Fairmont, Mark Hopkins, and Huntington, and the Pacific Union Club. The Powell flank is held by the Stanford Court Hotel, with Grace Cathedral and the Cathedral Apartments on the Jones Street side. The secondary defense on Sacramento Street consists of luxury apartments.

The only "neighbors" we see on this tour may be doormen or hotel guests alighting from a taxi—or the elderly rich assisted by nurses or companions.

The irony of this walk is that the most interesting characteristics can actually be noted by standing still—looking up to appreciate the architectural details high on the buildings and looking from eye level to enjoy the enjoyment of the cable car riders. Binoculars can add extended range to our sightings.

■ We begin at California and Leavenworth on the crest of Nob Hill. We go north on Leavenworth for a few yards and turn left into Acorn, one of San Francisco's most charming alleys, full of plants, color, and vitality. The cement alleyway is painted green, and a utility pole is wired around with green-painted clay pots full of flowers.

□ From Acorn, we turn north on Leavenworth to Sacramento Street. On the corner of Kimball Place, 1409 Sacramento Street is a large building in the Craftsman style. Ferns, a pine tree, and elephant ears at 5 Kimball help integrate the natural surroundings with urban concrete and brick.

□ East on Sacramento toward the Bay, the corner building at 1202-1206 Leavenworth is a 1910 Julia Morgan design of shingle and stucco, now beautifully covered with vines.

□ The foliage of the street trees adds a softness that makes this section of Sacramento Street very enticing. We pass other alleys—Golden, with its privet bushes and fuchsias, and LeRoy, with its symmetrical rows of trees. No. 10 Golden has spindles up to the top of the wall windows and terra cotta balusters.

□ Continuing east, we turn left on Jones. Grace Episcopal Cathedral School for Boys is on the corner of the square block that includes the diocesan house and the Cathedral itself. The school was built in 1966 for grades kindergarten through eighth.

☐ No. 1221 Jones is a luxury apartment and Le Club, at No. 1250, is a high society restaurant and nightclub. The Comstock Apartments at No. 1330 is named for the silver lode in Nevada that made the fortunes of James Fair and James Flood, two bonanza kings who had residences on Nob Hill.

■ At the intersection of Jones and Clay, we seem to be directly in front of the pyramid-shaped Transamerica Building, and on a clear day we can see right across the Bay to the Berkeley hills.

☐ Doubling back from the intersection, we go left into Pleasant. Some of the basement-skylight glass in the sidewalk at No. 16 is purple with age. No. 1140 is a Franco-Edwardian building with small-paned floor-length French doors.

☐ We make a right turn on Taylor to go south, and then left on Sacramento. In the sidewalk in front of 1162 Sacramento is a survey monument—inscribed under its cover with the precise latitude and longitude of this spot on the globe.

☐ Huntington Park, across the street, is an oasis of inviting benches, plantings, and sculpture. It was donated to the city in 1915 by Mrs. Collis P. Huntington, whose husband was one of the Big Four railroad barons who built mansions on Nob Hill.

☐ As we go along, the back of the landmark Pacific Union Club comes into view, one of the most exclusive men's clubs in the country. This brownstone building was built in 1886 for James Flood. Its exterior survived the quake and fire of 1906. In 1912, it was reconstructed and remodeled by Willis Polk. Legend has it that the bronze fence surrounding the property was once the full-time job of a maintenance man.

☐ We also see the white granite Fairmont Hotel. It was readied for its grand opening in 1906, when, on April 18 at 5:15 a.m. it was all but destroyed by the earthquake and fire (luckily, the fire insurance didn't expire until midnight!). The steel frame survived and a year later the hotel opened for business. The square block on which it stands was owned by James Fair, Flood's Comstock partner. A contemporary feature of the Fairmont is the exterior elevator, providing an unusual kinetic experience as one gradually ascends while watching the cityscape.

■ Continue east on Sacramento to Mason. The Brocklebank Apartments at 1000 Mason were built in 1924. Mythological beasts pose atop the elegant entrance.

☐ Down the hill, at the corner of Sacramento and Joice Street, is the Donaldina Cameron House, formerly the Chinese Presbyterian Mission Home. It was renamed in 1942 to honor the missionary who rescued young Chinese girls brought to San Francisco as factory slaves and prostitutes. Cameron House currently provides community recreational and social services. The clinker brick structure was built in 1881, then rebuilt in 1907 by Julia Morgan, one of the great

American architects. Morgan worked in the Bay Area from about 1905 to the 1930s, designed homes in the Craftsman style, and structures of grandeur and elegance such as the Union Bank on California Street and Hearst Castle at San Simeon.

☐ On Joice, turn right into the alley, and—happy day!—we have a stairway. It can also be reached from Pine between Powell and Stockton. Two light fixtures are in the center of the stairway and a large tree stands by one side. The concrete steps end at Pine in a rather graceful curve.

☐ We turn right on Pine. Above the high parapet in back of the Stanford Court Hotel is a sculptured cast-stone penguin by Beniamino Buffano, the impecunious artist and bohemian who captured the imagination of All San Francisco and, more importantly, the financial support of patrons. At the time of his death in 1970, many of his works were stored in warehouses. A Bufano Society of the Arts is working to establish a Bufano sculpture park. For the present, Bufano works are scattered here and there and one often comes upon them quite by chance—in the courtyard of the Academy of Sciences, in the North Terminal at the Airport, at the Phelan Street entrance to the Administration Building at San Francisco City College, or in the lobby of the Ordway Building in Oakland. The Mansion Bed and Breakfast on Sacramento and Laguna Streets has a large collection.

☐ We are now walking along the original granite retaining wall of the Stanford mansion, which was destroyed by the earthquake. The blocked entrance in the wall may have been for tradesmen. The tower with the finial marks the division between the Stanford and Hopkins properties. The wall divider is a visible expression of how social aggravations on the Hill were solved.

■ Turn right, going uphill on Mason. On the west side of the street is a graduated series of town houses, Nos. 831 to 840, Willis Polk designed these and they are a delightful counterfoil to the sumptuous structures on the hill.

☐ At the summit, the Mark Hopkins Hotel is a partner to the Fairmont Hotel across the street. Seeing the details, try to imagine what these buildings would look like with no ornamentation, or built with redwood. Impossible!

☐ We cross to No. 1001 California, a favorite. Behind the terra cotta columns and facade are ten apartments, each 2000 to 3000 square feet. The building feels cozier than do those surrounding it. Above the nameplate of Alexis, a well-known restaurant, is a bronze light fixture attached to a bracket in the shape of a basilisk, the fabulous serpent whose hissing drove away all other animals, and whose breath and look were fatal.

☐ Continuing west on California, we see the Huntington Hotel at No. 1075 on the corner of Taylor. "Less is more," says the adage; the restrained exterior belies what is considered by connoisseurs to be among the finest hotels in the city.

■ Across California Street is the main entrance to Huntington Park. On the side fronting Taylor is the rose-windowed entrance to Grace Cathedral, San Francisco's Gothic answer to Nôtre Dame of Paris.

☐ Episcopalian Grace Cathedral, designed by Lewis Hobart, was constructed from 1910 to 1928. The first cathedral, of wood, was built in 1906. As cathedrals traditionally are never finished, this second one is still under construction. Interior vaulting still needs to be done, and the murals by Antonio Sotomayor chronicling Cathedral and Parish history just recently were completed.

☐ As his inspiration for the present structure, Hobart used the cathedrals of Nôtre Dame, Amiens, and Ste. Chapelle. Acoustics are excellent, and concerts—sacred, secular, organ, choral, or jazz—are regularly presented. Duke Ellington, the famous jazz pianist, was commissioned by the diocese to compose a sacred piece which was performed at a concert in 1965. The quiet and elegant wrought iron-work on the gates to the Chapel of Grace on the south side nearest the California Street entrance was provided by Samuel Yellin.

☐ The land on which the Cathedral complex stands was donated to the Diocese by the Crocker family. Charles Crocker was the fourth of the Big Four railroad kings, and the fact that there is now a religious institution on his property is an irony to savor. When Crocker was frustrated by being unable to buy the adjoining lot to complete his purchase of the square block, he put up a forty-foot-high "spite fence" which cut off the sun and view from Nicholas Yung's house. Against Crocker's millions, Yung had no recourse. Crocker's heirs finally bought the property from Yung's estate.

☐ We now continue west on California to Leavenworth Street, completing our circle of the Hill and arriving back at our beginning.

Speaking of Intangibles

Every San Francisco neighborhood has its unique ambience—a distillation of the folklore and myths surrounding its beginning, and the character of the people who have lived there since.

Say "Nob Hill," and we think of resplendent wealth, Pacific Heights as well but with mansions, views, and spacious lots that seem more subdued. Russian Hill: a craggy, physically compact area, with creative people working at their crafts in flats and cottages tucked away among little streets and alleys, yet finding community and inspiration around them.

It's an image, it's atmosphere. We put out a hand to grasp it but it's intangible. Russian Hill, traditionally arty, may appeal to artists, but they can no longer afford to live there. They've moved to the poor man's Russian Hills—Noe Valley, Bernal Heights, Potrero Hill. Yet Russian Hill still has that intangible air.

■ We begin at Filbert and Polk, and walk east on Filbert. Already we are passing inviting, tucked-in homes, barely visible from the sidewalk—No. 1364, and especially No. 1338 with its long brick walk. At 2360 Larkin, the corner of Filbert, a copper whale rides atop the weathervane.

☐ The 1200 block of Filbert from Larkin to Hyde is composed mostly of Edwardian flats with bay windows on the two upper stories. This block has no trees, but next to No. 1252 is a terraced rock garden. Walking up the narrow private stairway of No. 1234 must be like walking up the keys of a grand piano. Other charming "tuck-ins" are on the other side of the street.

☐ Beginning at Hyde, we go down the Filbert sidewalk stairway. At the bottom we turn right on Leavenworth. A half block away, next to 2203 Leavenworth, is Havens Stairway, difficult to find but very charming. This is the only entrance and a worthwhile detour.

☐ The gardens alongside are part of properties belonging to individuals, who give them much attention. In early fall, figs from the beautiful mature tree at No. 14 cover the ground—obviously not the owner's favorite fruit.

☐ Returning to Leavenworth, we turn south toward Union. In the middle of the next block, next to 1934 Leavenworth, is Macondray Lane. Formerly known as Lincoln Street, Macondray Lane has a colorful history. Many writers have lived here; the single dwellings on the Lane have charm and variety. A medium-high condominium is the newest addition. We'll walk Macondray later.

VALLEJO STREET

■ We continue south to Green Street and turn left. Towering ahead are the Eichler Summit Apartments, 999 Green, built before the height limitation law was passed in 1970. Three long open oval shapes appear in the center of the tower, like huge exclamation points punctuating the end of a special block, the 1000 block of Green. This block completely escaped earthquake damage in 1906.

□ The oldest octagon house in San Francisco, dating from 1857, is at 1067 Green. This one is private. The Colonial Dames octagon, at Gough and Union, is open infrequently. The beautiful carriage house at the rear of No. 1055 Green is now used as living quarters. No. 1040 was once the home of the Folgers, whose fortune began with coffee. No. 1011, a brown-shingled house built after the earthquake, was designed around windows previously in the family's possession. No. 1039 is a square Italianate home surrounded by leafy trees.

□ At the end of the cul-de-sac is a large apartment house. We walk down the Green Street concrete stairway, with its bannisters in the middle, and turn right on Taylor.

□ Across from 1715 Taylor is the entrance to Ina Donna Coolbrith Park, given to the city by the Board of Education and dedicated in 1911. Ina Coolbrith (1841–1928) came to San Francisco at the age of ten in the first covered wagon train that traveled via the Beckwourth Pass in the high Sierra. Her father was a brother of Joseph Smith, the founder of the Mormon Church. She taught school for a time and later was a librarian at the Bohemian Club. She befriended many writers, and literary groups met at her home. In 1915, she was honored as poet laureate of California.

□ A few feet south from the park entrance is the Vallejo Stairway. Turning left, descend to Mason, turn right, then right again into Broadway. Here we see the dipping and rising of the land, extending to the highest hill south of us, Nob Hill (Walk 3). We're on the edge of Chinatown and Russian Hill.

■ The Broadway Tunnel under Russian Hill was proposed in 1874, permitted by city franchise in 1875, but not built and opened until 1952.

□ We walk on Broadway. The twin-towered Spanish National Church, Nuestra Señora de Guadalupe, with the mosaic tile figure of the Virgin, is at No. 906. The present structure was built in 1912 on the site of a wooden church dating from 1875. Today, masses are given in Spanish, English, and Cantonese, serving the ethnic variety in the adjoining neighborhoods.

□ Across the street at Himmelmann Place is a small park. At the corner of Broadway and Taylor is a high retaining wall with decorative edging along the top. We walk up the sidewalk stairway on the south side of Broadway for a better view of No. 1020, which is set up high and to the back of the property. This two-story brown shingle Craftsman style house was designed by Julia Morgan in 1909. We ascend the Florence Stairway next to 1032 Broadway: note the concrete wall topped with spindle decoration. There's something strange about this stairway. As we approach each landing, the landscape also seems to rise. Nos. 37 and 39 Florence are Pueblo Revival style with stucco exteriors and deep-set windows to deflect the sun.

☐ Nos. 40 and 42 Florence are also Julia Morgan designs, two of the many examples of the Craftsman style architecture on Russian Hill, the style espoused in the first quarter of the century by Morgan, Bernard Maybeck, Willis Polk, and Ernest Coxhead as an antidote to the excesses and formalism of Victorian architecture. The emphasis was on the natural: redwood shingles, protruding eaves instead of bracketed cornices, and gabled roofs. These homes were set into the property to merge with the slope of the land. Natural greenery is an important part of the design; the outdoors seems to come inside and to extend the living area outside.

☐ We continue down the Florence Stairway to Vallejo, and cross the street to Russian Hill Place.

■ It's hard to believe that Russian Hill possesses such a concentration of bewitching little streets in such a small area! Craftsman houses are the perfect style for the nooks and crannies of Russian Hill. Nos. 1, 3, 5, and 7 Russian Hill Place are Willis Polk houses of 1913. We walk around the lane, then double back left to Vallejo, and walk on the south side. Nos. 1015 and 1017 Vallejo are Willis Polks. He also redesigned No. 1045, which had been part of the Horatio Livermore ranch-estate on the Vallejo cliff.

☐ We head east and down the Vallejo Stairway to Taylor. We turn left on Taylor and walk until we come to the other end of Macondray Lane.

☐ One of the charms of Macondray Lane is the variety of materials used on the stairway—wood, cobblestones, and brick. The trees and shrubbery in varying shades of green reinforce the dignity of this area.

☐ Where Macondray meets Jones we turn left on Green—we've been along here—and turn right onto Leavenworth.

☐ At Union Street, we walk west. No. 1150 Union was built in the 1930s. It is white with an interesting decorative motif of curved leaves.

☐ The many neighborhood stores near Hyde and Union make shopping here a multi-stop session. Marcel and Henri, butcher and charcuterie, have been serving the community for more than twenty years. The Home Drug store at 1200 Union has been in the same family since 1912, and still serves customers who first came to them in the 1930s. The Searchlight has been a grocery for sixty years under various owners. Le Valet, a cleaning establishment, has been owned by the same person since 1952; people from all over the city bring their leather and suede here. A repair shop, the original Swensen's ice-cream parlor, an auto service, and more cleaners, are all within reach.

☐ These shopkeepers symbolize the continuity and stability that contribute to the intangible that is Russian Hill.

☐ We continue west on Union to Polk, turn right to Filbert, and are at our beginning.

San Francisco Architectural Signatures

From the vantage point of Pacific Heights, Russian Hill appears to be shaped like a shoe with a square toe. Significant! In many places, Russian Hill is inaccessible except to walkers.

The Craftsman homes designed by Northern California architects Julia Morgan, Willis Polk, and Bernard Maybeck in the early 1900s blend well into this terrain, where irregularly shaped deep lots abound, making some houses—the kind that we call "tuck-ins"—invisible from the street. These tuck-ins are as much the city's architectural signature as the loftier towers also to be seen on this walk.

■ Our starting point is on Polk Street where the Greenwich Street hill begins its sharp rise toward Larkin. The empty lot on the corner, now overgrown with mallow, fennel, and mustard, is scheduled to be the site of condominiums. Neighbors protested the height of the proposed building and advocated the preservation of the large Monterey cypress trees.

☐ We walk north on Polk for one block and then turn right on Lombard. The 1200 block on Lombard beautifully illustrates construction-on-a-slant. No. 1275 is a brown shingle tuck-in. Nos. 1263 to 1257 are Italianates, with ivy on the walls adding warmth to the buildings. No. 1249 is a remodeled flat-front Italianate, a tuck-in high on the hill.

☐ At 1256 Lombard, we turn left to walk down the Culebra Terrace Stairway, according to the hard-to-see sign on the side of No. 1246. This is a stairway with three landings, 29 steps with a coda of two.

☐ Culebra is a charming alley of flats and single dwellings. The podocarpus tree and well-tended shrubbery attest to gardeners about. No. 60 has a terrazzo stairway and interesting little tiles. Nos. 25 and 35 are simple cottages. No. 23 was built in 1911.

☐ We come out of Culebra onto the Chestnut Street cul-de-sac, bear east, and walk up a wide stairway with gardens on either side shadowed by Monterey pines.

■ Forty-eight steps bring us to a landing that begins a U-formation. We use the right-hand stairway, and walk another 64 steps up to Larkin Street. Looking back, we see down the Greenwich corridor to the north central side of San Francisco, and the two dominant forms of that part of the city—the unmistakable dome of the Palace of Fine Arts

CHESTNUT STREET

(Walk 8, Pacific Heights) and the Golden Gate Bridge.

☐ We turn right on Larkin. A house on the corner has a brass plaque: "2677 Larkin at Chestnut Street." We wish they had included the year the house was built and the architect's name.

☐ We continue up one block. At the southeast corner of Lombard, walk up a stairway into the Alice Marble Tennis Courts, dedicated in 1967. This is Water Department land, and the reservoir underneath supplies many blocks of houses. Here is a bench and an uncluttered view of Marin toward the northwest. We continue on the footpath to the sound of tennis balls against tennis racquets above us until we arrive at the Greenwich Stairs. Go up instead of down, a very easy 27 steps past the upper landing with benches and a mosaic tile wall. Continue another, hardly noticeable, 27 steps up onto the sidewalk, and the view of the tennis players below.

☐ We walk down 26 steps to Hyde, then turn left to face Alcatraz, another San Francisco signature. Stop a moment at Hyde and Lombard, a splendid place to see the Hyde Street cable car lurching along with its standing-room-only crowd of passengers. With the conductor's full approval they alight en masse with their cameras pointed toward Alcatraz, the Bay Bridge, and Treasure Island. At the clang of the cable car bell, they rush aboard once more to coast down to the next landing on their way to Aquatic Park, while we continue walking north on Hyde.

☐ Highrise has struck again—at Hyde and Chestnut, and yet again at Chestnut and Larkin! It's too late to complain.

■ Across the street is the roof of another city reservoir. Straight ahead is the Hyde Street Pier with its famous collection of historic ships. It's a part of the National Maritime Museum. We pass the Norwegian Seamen's Church at 2454 Hyde. (The Norwegian government sponsors a seamen's social service at 2501 Vallejo Street, an indication of the number of Norwegian sailors who make port here.)

☐ We walk down three steps to Francisco Street, and turn right. This cul-de-sac is a favorite. The large homes here, in a variety of styles and set on several levels of land, command enviable views from either side of the street.

☐ No. 828 Francisco has a bay of leaded windows with octagonal inserts, a modified mansard roof, and beautiful copper chimney stacks that have taken on a greenish cast over the years. A fence espaliered with roses follows the slope of the hill. No. 825 is one of the oldest homes in San Francisco. It was constructed of timber salvaged from ships abandoned in the Bay during the Gold Rush.

☐ We stand on the parapet next to 800 Francisco to gaze at the variety of architectural shapes and signatures that are part of a San Franciscan's daily eyeful. Beginning with the abundant sword-shaped leaves of a palm tree at the lower corner of the street, take in the rectangular towers of the Bay Bridge, the cylindrical Coit Tower, the cone-shaped towers of Saint Peter and Paul's Church in North Beach, the square Romanesque tower of the San Francisco Art Institute, and the Transamerica Pyramid.

☐ Follow the retaining wall to bear right and south to Chestnut, where we turn right. Turn left into Montclair and walk up 28 steps to a distinguished group of homes and gardens. At the corner next to No. 4, we are at Lombard Street, where drivers enjoy the unusual ride down the curviest street in the country.

☐ However, we turn right to go up a straight 95 steps, so comfortably that we know the stairway follows the ideal formula: twice the riser (the height) plus the tread (the width) should equal 26 inches.

☐ At the top, we continue west on Lombard, back of the Alice Marble Tennis Court past a large lot empty of house but full of wild mustard.

☐ At Larkin, turn left. No. 2531 is a stick-style Italianate with a picket fence.

☐ At Greenwich, turn right down a grooved sidewalk. A retaining wall around the remains of a recently leveled Victorian house is next to No. 1354. No. 1356 lifts our spirits again with its interesting angular design of concrete landings and steps—as we arrive at the point we began.

FORT MASON

Pivoting Rakishly around the Four-Tiered Ellipse in Two Movements

On this walk, we explore some of the extensive municipal and federal recreational areas of San Francisco that are still evolving along the northern waterfront, including new stairways. Here the atmosphere is highly energized and the history more apparent than in other neighborhoods.

As we progress from the Marina Green to the Hyde Street Pier, we can appreciate how this land became a focus for federal military installations and is now well on its way to becoming a focus for National Park ownership for peaceful purposes.

Beginning at the Marina Green, the area is one big beautiful pivotal platform, from which we can set forth afoot in almost any direction—east to North Beach and Telegraph Hill, southeast toward Downtown, west to the Palace of Fine Arts, or southwest toward Pacific Heights.

The sun's rays, intensified by reflections from the water, bestow warmth and good cheer on everything and everybody. The sounds coming from everywhere on the Marina Green—hummingbirds chipping, song sparrows singing, gulls crying, dogs barking, people laughing, an occasional street vendor sending up a sales holler, all to the music of the Bay swishing in the background—turn this into a celebration walk. Here, when there's sun and color and kites and games and laughter, we have to say, "Happy day, everyone!"

■ We begin at Scott Street and Marina Boulevard, where the Marina Green continues the tradition of amusement intended when it was born from the sea as the site of the extravagant 1915 Panama-Pacific International Exposition.

☐ Follow the Promenade along the water, past the mysterious degaussing station, to the exercise parcourse placards at the end. Fisherfolk might be tempted to go north, but continue on the path that curves around Yacht Harbor, thinking all the while that it's a good thing some boats don't know their names (for instance, *Winky-Dinky* and *Lots of Lox*). Alongside in the water are coots, western grebes, and mallards. Mallow, oxalis, and crown of jewels are blooming beside the walkway.

☐ We pass by Gas House Cove just before we enter the first tier of Fort Mason.

☐ Fort Mason is now part of the Golden Gate National Recreation

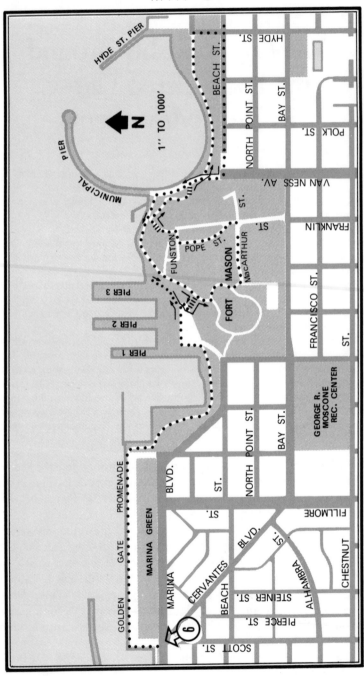

6 □ Pivoting Rakishly Around the Four-Tiered Ellipse

Area, established in 1972. Here we can trace a nonstop evolving historical line (not necessarily straight) from 1797 to the present, from Spanish and American military fortifications to a section of the most popular urban park in the United States. (As this is written, the Fort Mason area is being informally relandscaped; walkers are advised to be undaunted, and to use these itineraries as suggestions.)

☐ Urban parks, a relatively new concept in national park design, bring parks to where people are. As we walk through Fort Mason, an area of about 300 acres, the idea of melding nature and city is manifest.

■ Enter Fort Mason on the lower level (Tier 1), a point of embarcation for men and supplies from the turn of the century. The buildings alongside the piers were used by the Army through demobilzation after World War II, and are now used for recreational and cultural activities. Several nonprofit community organizations are headquartered at Fort Mason in exchange for reasonable rents. The Magic Theater produces plays that merit national attention. The Mexican Museum is a unique north-of-the-border institution. Greens is a very popular restaurant with Tassajara Zen vegetation cooking.

☐ In the parking lot to our right, the Beniamino Bufano statue of granite and mosaic is dedicated to "Peace," but seems singularly unrelated to its environment. The Society of Friends of Bufano hopes that all his scattered sculptures will one day be part of a sculpture park. Bufano (1898–1970) was a favorite San Francisco personality supported by various benefactors such as the Powell Street restaurant for which he designed and executed a mosaic wall in return for a lifetime of meals.

☐ We pass Buildings A, B , C, and D; and Piers 1 and 2. Permanently stationed at Pier 3 is a World War II Liberty Ship, the *Jeremiah O'Brien*, built in a record 56 days in 1943.

☐ Building F houses the Actors Ark Theater. Opposite, a mural entitled "Positively Fourth Street" depicts a surreal San Francisco scene which includes a freeway inhabited by animals and driverless automobiles.

■ As we continue our walk along the wall, note the stern of *The Galilee*, a Tahitian trading vessel built in 1891 and in use until 1920. Next to it is an exhibit of the *Textite*, an experimental underwater habitat outfitted for six scientists; it is to be used to study the effects of radioactive waste dumping on the marine environment. The Oceanic Society has its offices nearby.

☐ Opposite Building E is a stairway where, as we walk up the first series of steps, we see hummingbirds dipping and revolving around one another.

☐ Continuing on up, we arrive at Pier 4 and walk over to the Great Meadow on our right, retracing the long-forgotten footsteps of hundreds of men, women, and children who lived here in tents after losing their homes in 1906. Refugee Camp No. 5 extended beyond the meadow to the site of the present Safeway store to the west. This part of Fort Mason has been dedicated to the late San Francisco Congressman Philip Burton, father of many national parklands, including GGNRA.

☐ This plateau affords a clear view of Marina Boulevard stretching toward the ocean, Golden Gate Bridge, and the Palace of Fine Arts.

■ Walk to Park Headquarters in Building 201, on MacArthur Street immediately south of the Community Gardens. No. 201 was built in 1901 as a hospital for the military. After the earthquake, it was one of the busiest places in the city, used as a lying-in hospital and providing emergency care for victims. According to legend, eight babies were born at Fort Mason the night after the quake.

☐ Fort Mason was first the headquarters for General Funston, who put San Francisco under martial law to prevent looting and then, under General Greely, the center for relief-supply distribution. At this time, the Navy fireboat anchored off Fort Mason pumped water from the Bay to the fire engines along Van Ness Avenue. Mayor Schmitz moved his office to Fort Mason to coordinate civil and military authority. In the years following 1906, Building 201 was used as administrative headquarters for Fort Mason. Among the officers who served here during World War II was a second lieutenant in charge of tracking down missing shipments; his name was Ronald Reagan.

☐ Walk in front of No. 201. The tile-roof military housing to our right dates from World War II. We make a left turn to Pope. Near the corner is the Chapel (1942) and the starting place of the Conversation-Pace Gamefield sponsored by the San Francisco Senior Center. Various exercises are paced slowly enough to allow for conversation.

☐ We walk into the Community Garden driveway to explore the various garden plots. This is one of 54 community gardens in the city. Space is available to anyone living in the Fort Mason area, but there is a long waiting list. Back of the gardens is the historic parade ground, where regiments marched and stood for inspection. The hostel at the end of Pope is the most recent addition to community facilities at Fort Mason. The place is clean and inviting, and some of its guests are lolling about on the grass.

☐ At the hostel, we turn right on Funston, a few steps to the head of Franklin Street, marked by a Monterey cypress. This part of Fort Mason contains military housing dating from the 1850s. These structures function in their original capacity until their future transfer to the Department of the Interior. The officers' housing on the east side of Pope Street originated as squatters' homes, put up in the 1850s by prominent San Franciscans who knew valuable real estate when they saw it.

FORT MASON

■ High pro- and anti-slavery feelings in California culminated in the famous Terry-Broderick duel in 1859. Senator David Broderick, shot by the hot-tempered pro-slavery Judge David Terry near Lake Merced, died here at Fort Mason in the home of a friend. The Army repossessed the squatters' homes (after all, this was originally Army property) and began building up fortifications in anticipation of the Confederate onslaught.

☐ We walk north, on an inviting path. To the left is a plaque noting the site of the Batería San José, a Spanish seacoast defense battery located here in 1797. It was built to protect the anchorage at Yerba Buena, the oldest commercial section in San Francisco around what is today Montgomery and Jackson. We are standing on what is known as Black Point Lookout, so called because of the shade provided by the laurel trees.

☐ The Bay was theoretically well-defended against hostile fleets and, later, aircraft, but no one has yet attacked. At one time or another there were Spanish or American coastal batteries at the three forts on the Marin Headlands, across the Golden Gate on the Presidio cliffs, on Alcatraz and Angel Island, and here at Fort Mason. The best-preserved of these antiquated defenses is Fort Point, the Civil War fort under the arch of the Golden Gate Bridge.

☐ Continuing on the path, we go down to the planned picnic grounds, to be built on battery platforms dating back to the Civil War. The Park is reconstructing the Black Point area, with or without the old stairway.

☐ Those of us who would rather sunbathe on the green may return to the hostel area and down Magazine Street to the promenade, then down the stairway to Pier 1, through the pier-area parking lot, and back to the Green. We whose feet ache for more stairway walking may continue on the path to a pair of stairs, exploring the cliffside and admiring the Bay views.

☐ We find ourselves at the foot of Van Ness Avenue. The curved concrete wall of Aquatic Park, formerly known as Black Point Cove, was part of the San Jose Point Military Reservation that became Fort Mason in 1882.

■ The following walk is so full of stoppable places that one must simply go where mood directs.

☐ To the left is Pumping Station No. 2, built to supply water in case of earthquake and fire. Across the street, restrooms are housed in a round white structure with incised wavy lines near the roof line to simulate ocean waves—another example of the Streamline Moderne style of the 1930s. The duplicate of this structure is at Hyde Street and Jefferson, also a restroom.

☐ We promenade along the water, and walk up the amphitheatrical steps to watch birds and swimmers.

☐ The shiplike Maritime Museum to the right, opened in 1950, exhibits old ship models and other artifacts and prints, and contains a library of books relating to maritime history. The Moderne building was erected in 1939 as a WPA project.

☐ We walk east on Jefferson toward the Hyde Street Pier. As we approach the "working" fisherman's area, the wooden buildings look weatherbeaten and the atmosphere begins to change.

☐ Continue to the Hyde Street Pier where historic ships are docked and one can take an imaginary trip on the *Eureka*, a passenger ferry, the *Thayer*, a sailing schooner that carried lumber, salmon, and codfish, or the *Wapama*, a steam schooner for cargo and passengers.

☐ Across Hyde Street Victorian Park practically sends the message, "Come on over!" Besides the gazebo and flowerway, the cable car turntable is here, with jolly crowds waiting to board. Go south and turn right on Beach Street. The Wine Museum of San Francisco, only museum of its kind in North America, was once located in the Fromm-Sichel Building on the southeast corner. The beautiful wrought-iron gates open onto an aggregate patio that has raised beds of flowers and trees, benches, and a mosaic fountain in the corner. The inviting atmosphere continues into the museum, where the collections of glasses, sculpture, and prints provide an intriguing examination of social history as it celebrates the grape. One of the more amusing exhibits is the corkscrew collection of Brother Timothy, cellarmaster of the Christian Brothers Winery in Napa Valley.

■ We reverse our course and go west on Beach. Among the outdoor stalls of jewelry, leather belts, and stained-glass windows, the owner of a parrot and a macaw allows his trained birds to sit on the arms of visitors, sometimes to bestow a kiss on a surprised benefactor.

☐ In another block is Ghirardelli Square, a chocolate factory built in 1893 and converted in 1967 to a well-designed complex of specialty shops and stairways. This is an excellent place for coffee, lunch, or browsing.

☐ Several factories were located in this area in the latter half of the 1800s. The Selby Smelting Works, which refined silver from the Comstock, was here. The old Pioneer Woolen Mill is now part of Ghirardelli Square.

☐ The Neptune Baths, whose members swam in the Bay, was an active organization until 1890. William Ralston, the fabulous owner of silver mines and the Bank of California, was a daily Bay swimmer. In August 1875, the day after the bank closed its doors because of Ralston's embezzlement, he drowned just off Aquatic Park.

☐ A plaque commemorates the *San Carlos*, which on August 5, 1775 was the first ship into San Francisco Bay.

☐ We continue west to Van Ness. We can decide to end our walk by stepping aboard the Muni's No. 30 to Broderick and Beach (at the Marina Green), or we can return via the Fort Mason Promenade at the foot of Van Ness.

MAP D

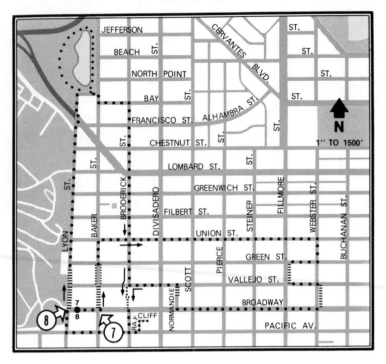

7 □ Stairway to a Missing House
8 □ Tripping Lightly

Stairway to a Missing House

When the first cable car went over Nob Hill in 1878, the development of Pacific Heights, the ridge across the Polk-Van Ness Valley, followed soon after. Then as now, the views of the Bay were extraordinary. Although a precipitous 370 feet above sea level, the Heights had many wide, flat lots for the large homes only the wealthy could afford.

Architectural styles abound: elaborate Queen Anne Victorians of the 1890s, Mission Revival, Edwardian, mock Chateau, and imitations of Le Petit Trianon, Marie Antoinette's palace (the Spreckels' mansion at 2935 Washington Street).

Pacific Heights is an excellent area to practice sightings of architectural details—general, singular, and humorous.

■ We begin at Broadway and Baker Street. No. 2890 Broadway on the northeast corner was built in 1889 by Bliss and Faville, famous for classical government buildings. (A few blocks away on Broadway toward the end of this walk other Bliss and Faville homes invite comparison.)

☐ We walk north down the two-block-long Baker Stairway. Dense plantings on both sides hem the walk in and the tread-to-riser proportion makes these steps seem steeper than they really are.

☐ Entering Vallejo Street from the stairs, walk into a cul-de-sac with handsome river stones embedded on the slope. The large home at 2901 Baker on the corner of Vallejo, built in 1886, is a combination of Mediterranean and Mission styles. No. 2891 Vallejo, with its stained-glass windows, might have been a church. Note the cobblestone tree troughs in the sidewalk around city trees. No. 2881 has the narrowest second-story window I've ever seen.

☐ The lower section of the Baker Stairway is lighter and more cheerful. Open space around the comfortable stairs makes this a happy, bouncy descent.

☐ Continue to Union and turn right. No. 2784 Union is a rough stucco structure, an example of Pueblo Revival architecture. No. 2735 is a gray Queen Anne row house with a spindled arch over the front door. The front door has special features: a row of six buttons and a quarter sunburst on either side. Under fish-scale shingles at the very peak of the gable are rows of alternating square butt shingles.

☐ The Balein Apartments features art-glass windows and a whale weathervane. The flats at 2663–2641 Union carry out several architectural ideas popular in 1870. The lots on which they are built are unusually narrow so the buildings are of necessity narrow and tall with bay windows and balconies in a rhythmic, repetitive pattern.

■ A missing house? A stairway to a missing house? There is space for a house between 2535 and 2559 Union Street; a stairway, a partial retaining wall, some terracing in the back, and a few years' growth of shrubbery are in evidence, but no house. Puzzled? It'll show up.

☐ No. 2460, with its mansard roof and sunbonnet gable, was built in 1892. Open balconies at No. 2255 almost overwhelm the central front stairway.

☐ The Episcopal Church of the Virgin at 2325 Union, built in 1891, was known as the Cow Hollow Church. (The Cow Hollow walk is No. 8.) Past the gate, there is a fish pond in the courtyard; the high steeple landmark of St. Vincent de Paul Church on Green at Steiner is just visible.

☐ From Steiner to Gough, Union is a long street of retail stores—bakeries, antique shops, restaurants, and bars. The Victorian houses in this section were deteriorating badly until 1963 when No. 1980 Union and adjoining buildings were transformed from three residences into two restaurants and nine stores. Beverly Willis, designer and architect, set the tone and style of the street by putting retail stores in charming Victorian homes. The Union Street Association worked assiduously to maintain and promote the coherent look the street now has.

☐ No. 2237 is a U-shaped building with two Queen Anne towers, and a witch's cap and finials for a comic touch. No. 2129, at the southeast corner of Union and Fillmore, is a wonderful Edwardian building with dentils and egg-and-dart details along the top and a moulding of banded laurel leaves with berries at the bottom.

■ We turn right on Webster. No. 2550 was built by Willis Polk in 1896 for William Bourn, who at various times was the head of the Spring Valley Water Company, Pacific Gas and Electric, and the Empire Mining Company in Grass Valley. Bourn hired Polk to design Filoli, his garden estate in Woodside, now part of the National Trust for Historic Preservation. No. 2550 sports a pineapple finial, architectural symbol of hospitality.

☐ On Green Street, we turn right again. No.2160, a landmark, was built in 1867 for Leander Sherman of Sherman-Clay music stores. It was designed especially for musical gatherings, and artists such as Madame Schumann-Heink and Ignace Jan Paderewski performed there. In the back is a rather elaborate carriage house with mansard roof and shingles in alternating patterns of diamonds and octagons. Some of the walk lights in front of the carriage house show the purple tint of oxidation. The present owner is attempting to get permission for a bed-and-breakfast inn here. It would be a charming one.

☐ On Fillmore we turn left. We see St. Vincent de Paul Church to the west. Its square tower is copper-clad. Masses are in English except for an Italian mass once a month.

☐ Someone has replaced a lion's head with a steer's head on the frame below the bay window at 2200 Green, a rough stucco structure.

■ Walk the sidewalk steps up Fillmore from Green to Vallejo. No. 2323, designed by Henry Gutterson and completed in 1959, now houses the Vedanta Society.

☐ We turn left one block back to Webster where we walk up the stairway to Broadway. This is one of San Francisco's most famous views. Here, two estates once belonging to the Flood family are now private schools. In 1898, No. 2120 was built as the residence of James Flood, one of the bonanza kings of the Comstock, and is now the Sarah Dix Hamlin School for Girls. The gardens and tennis courts extend down the depth of the lot to 2129 Vallejo, where an addition to Miss Hamlin's school was built in 1965. The two buildings are connected by a stairway.

☐ Walking west on Broadway, we come to No. 2223, the James Leary Flood mansion, designed by Bliss and Faville in a Renaissance piazza style and completed in 1915. The exterior of Tennessee marble and limestone is considered by connoisseurs to be the best stonework in San Francisco. In 1939, this mansion was deeded by Mrs. Maud Flood to the Order of the Sacred Heart, and is now a convent school. The two other parts of the school complex are No. 2252, the Stuart Hall for Boys, and 2200 Broadway.

☐ No. 2520 is a mock French chateau, with a separate ceremonial staircase up to the front door, which is on the second floor, a whimsical touch.

☐ We reach Broadway and Fillmore, one of San Francisco's most famous views, and continue down and up Broadway to Normandie Terrace, a cul-de-sac with personality, and down a relatively unknown stairway to Vallejo. From here, two options are possible: return up this stairway to continue west on Broadway to our starting point at Baker, or descend, turn west, and walk up the Broderick Stairway to Broadway. Our beginning is just one block away.

LYON STREET

PRESIDIO WALL

Tripping Lightly

After the 1906 Earthquake, there was an exodus from the devastation of Nob Hill to Pacific Heights; it has always been a wealthy, stable neighborhood.

Most of the mansions on Nob Hill belonged to men who made their fortunes in the Comstock silver mines in Nevada or from the building of the Southern Pacific Railroad. The Pacific Heights mansions were built by men whose fortunes were made from a variety of enterprises that dealt more directly with San Francisco.

Henry Casebolt built carriages and invented the cable car grip that made Pacific Heights accessible and facilitated the growth of this neighborhood, Louis Sloss and Daniel Koshland were merchants of grain and groceries, Leander Sherman sold sheet music and musical instruments, and the Roos brothers supplied much of the general merchandise and dry goods.

Cow Hollow was the pasture and dairy land of the City until a cholera epidemic at the turn of the century forced the dairy industry to Glen Park, a less populated area south of Twin Peaks. In the 1960s, Cow Hollow's Union Street was the first shopping street in the city to systematically renovate and recycle dilapidated Victorian homes into retail stores, offices, and the like, becoming a model for other projects throughout the Bay Area.

The Marina rose as the palpable expression of hope and determination for the city's rebirth following the earthquake and fire. The Marina was built on landfill planned as the site of the spectacular Panama-Pacific Exposition of 1915, which celebrated the completion of the Panama Canal. The fair went on for a year and many people still remember it as the most beautiful of the several world's fairs held in the United States. When it isn't on tour, a miniature replica of the Exposition's magnificent buildings, including the Tower of Jewels and the Fountain of Energy, may be seen at the Presidio Museum in the Presidio.

The Marina today is a friendly composition of peoples. The harbor and the Golden Gate National Recreation Area contribute to its physical beauty, while many storekeepers along thriving Chestnut Street never forget the names of old customers, or discontinue home delivery.

■ We begin at Lyon Street and Broadway with a splendid view of the Palace of Fine Arts, the stunning, columned Romanesque rotunda below us, the Marin hills serving as a backdrop.

☐ We're going to walk north on Lyon for more than nine blocks along the edge of the Presidio. We begin our descent toward the Marina through a wall on Lyon Street and down a stone stairway. The 130 steps come to a rest on Vallejo before resuming with another 124 across the street.

☐ Five and a half blocks along, cross Richardson at Francisco Street and continue on Lyon to the Palace of Fine Arts. Here people always seem to be picnicking and sunning, with wedding parties being photographed and ducks being fed. It's an irresistibly romantic location.

☐ We bear left around the theater to the Exploratorium, a museum where adults and children may participate actively—touching, seeing, listening, moving—in experiments that illustrate scientific principles. This was the brainchild of physicist Frank Oppenheimer and his late wife, Jackie, who envisioned it as a place where visitors can explore their perceptions of the physical world. High schoolers do the explaining where necessary. The Exploratorium is one of the most vital museums in the city, and a favorite.

☐ At the Exploratorium's Baker Street exit, we turn into the path that fronts some Baker Street homes and circles the lagoon among the Monterey cypresses. We sight a European widgeon, a bufflehead, and some coots. The area on the south side of the lagoon is known as Walter S. Johnson Park. A plaque on a fluted planter records that Johnson, a millionaire who lived across the street, helped preserve this Bernard Maybeck building, the only architectural survivor of the 1915 Fair's many temporary structures.

■ The Spanish-style architecture that is typical of the Marina seems to reflect all the sunlight. Walking two blocks east on Bay to Broderick, turn right and walk toward Chestnut, the Marina's shopping street.

☐ We cross Lombard, a major artery, to walk seven blocks uphill on Broderick. Here the houses are eclectic but architecturally sound. No. 2821 and the house next door were the earliest houses on the block, dating from about 1907.

☐ At Broderick and Vallejo, we come to an overpass stairway that leads into the driveway and garage of 2798 Broderick. The landscaping here counteracts the steepness of a hill beautifully—three pine trees planted among large riverbed rocks laid out in a pleasing pattern in the center of the street with cobblestones outlining the margins. Toward Broadway, Broderick becomes a miniature "curly Lombard Street."

☐ Up a stairway of 19 steps plus a sidewalk of 21 steps, we arrive at 2800 Broadway, a 1907 Jacobean style mansion designed by Willis Polk. It features early Renaissance stone archways and leaded windows; a magnolia tree blooms out front. No. 2801 Broadway, with its Corinthian columns, cries out for cascading greenery to clothe the bare walls.

☐ From this height, it is hard to believe we recently left the Palace of Fine Arts.

■ We continue on Broderick. At Pacific, we detour left for about fifty feet for a look at Raycliff Terrace, a charming cul-de-sac of six houses designed by contemporary architects.

☐ We turn around and walk west on Pacific. The El Drisco Hotel, built in 1903, was probably the earliest hotel to be situated in a residential area. It has been under the same ownership since 1944 and carries on a tradition of personal service to the guests in its fifty rooms.

☐ This being such prime and coveted land, the two empty lots next to No. 2950 come as a shock. No. 2950 is a "tuck-in" house, placed at a distance from the sidewalk. An unusual variance gives three houses at No. 3070 one driveway with entrances both on Pacific and Lyon streets.

☐ By turning downhill at Lyon, we reach Broderick and our beginning.

MAP E

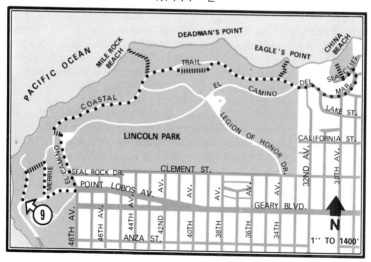

9 ☐ The James Milestone Walk

The James Milestone Walk

This walk goes through the westernmost section of San Francisco, an area closely identified with Adolph Sutro who arrived in the city in 1850 from Aix-La-Chapelle. He's a favorite San Francisco pioneer.

Sutro was trained as an engineer but worked in the tobacco business until the silver strike in the Comstock mines. Floods and noxious fumes had almost halted operations when Sutro designed a tunnel that would have drained and ventilated the mines, not only saving the lives of miners but increasing output as well. The owners, Ralston, Fair, and Flood, saw Sutro as a threat to their profits and refused to finance the tunnel project.

Sutro was persistent, obtained financial help from the East, sold his invention, and invested the profits in San Francisco real estate. Some books say he eventually owned one-twelfth of the city, including a portion of Rancho Miguel that comprised the areas now known as Glen Park and Diamond Heights. Later he deeded the 26 acres on Mount Sutro to the University of California for its big Medical Center.

An avid horticulturist, Sutro planted everywhere. Entomologists and botanists decry his selection of non-native plants because they altered the area's ecology. It's difficult to take a walk in San Francisco without being aware of his influence. He was responsible for foresting the Presidio, Fort Mason, Mount Sutro, and Yerba Buena Island (the mound of land that anchors the Bay Bridge) with eucalyptus.

In addition to greening the city, he established the Sutro Library (now at San Francisco State University) which specializes in local history and genealogy.

Adolph Sutro was a David among Goliaths. In 1894, he was elected mayor of San Francisco on the Populist platform, opposing the Southern Pacific Railroad and its policy of monopoly. And while the other multimillionaires lived on Nob Hill and in Pacific Heights, Sutro built his seaside castles in the Richmond district. His Sutro Heights home was a twenty-one-acre estate of sculpture-crowded landscaped gardens. The house has long been gone but the garden is open to the public as part of the Golden Gate National Recreation Area.

One of Sutro's best-known contributions to the city was the famous Cliff House, indeed, two of three Cliff Houses. The first two (1863–1894 and 1896–1907) were destroyed. The second and third were built by Sutro, and the surviving third has been much modernized and changed since 1950.

Another popular recreation spot associated with this interesting character was Sutro Baths: six indoor salt-water pools and seats for 7000 spectators, with palms and Egyptian relics in the plant conservatories—truly a DeMille spectacle.

(*Note:* The following is an extra-sweater walk. The temperature can change capriciously. Also, those who forget binoculars will be sorry.)

■ The walk starts behind 902 Point Lobos Avenue (Louis' Restaurant as this is written) on a footpath beside a yellow railing. Below are the ruins of Sutro Baths, closed in 1952 and destroyed by fire in 1966. Broken columns, fragments of tile mosaic, and the emptied pool area extend toward the ocean. The eroded sandstone setting and the off-shore Sea Rocks add to the melancholy drama of the site. The whole seems right for the unfolding of a Greek tragedy.

☐ From Sutro Baths, we walk up a sand ladder that adds a little bit of Holland to San Francisco. James Milestone, a ranger with the Golden Gate National Recreation Area, had seen a similar ladder on a dune north of Amsterdam and adapted the idea for Land's End, where it was built in 1981 under his supervision. Since it is probably the only one in the United States, it is worth describing.

☐ The rungs are wooden poles two inches in diameter and four feet long. Holes drilled at each end are secured to wire cables that are the main stringers of the ladder. These cables, each about 25 feet long, are tied into four-by-four posts sunk about five feet into the soil. The rungs are spaced about 18 inches apart, which is the length of a normal footstep, and make it very easy to get up a hill.

☐ This sand ladder lies on the surface of the slope, the downhill side of it loose so it can be easily picked up and shaken out if it gets buried in the sand. Each rung acts as a dam to hold back sand. Most people walking up and down put their weight on the rung instead of on the sand between the rungs.

☐ The sand ladder is succeeded by a stairway made of railroad ties, a capacious eight feet wide, to allow room for the large number of people who visit the Golden Gate Recreation Area, the most popular of the National Parks—in 1980, it had 1.9 million visitors!

☐ Plants native to the sand dunes are being encouraged by park botanists. Along the way, we see dune tansy, blue bush lupine, beach primrose, and coyote bush. The area sometimes suffers landslides during heavy winter rains, so parts of the trails may be closed. We just walk on the alternate path indicated when necessary.

■ We continue up the stairway to the Merrie Way parking lot, and south on to Point Lobos Avenue, turning north at El Camino Del Mar, which we follow to the stairway down to the Point Lobos lookout. This stairway is made of recycled railroad ties from the never-completed Belt Line Railroad. The chain rails are from some of the historic ships at the Maritime Museum.

☐ We join the Coastal Trail at Point Lobos and follow it to the lookout at Mile Rock Beach and descend the stairway for a look at the automated Mile Rock Lighthouse.

☐ On a clear day much of the Golden Gate National Recreation Area can be seen across the Gate: from west to east past the Headlands of Marin—Tennessee Cove, Rodeo Beach, Bird Island, the lighthouse at

LAND'S END

Point Bonita, Bonita Cove, Conzelman Road, Point Diablo, Kirby Beach, and the Golden Gate Bridge. Lands End is the outcropping of rock to our right.

☐ We walk back up the stairway and continue eastward to Painted Rock Point, a Coast Guard Marker, then bear right along the stairway reconstructed by the Young Adult Conservation Corps. It is close to Dead Man's Point, a name that graphically describes the fate of some who wanted a close-up view of the formation.

☐ We continue along the trail to the Eagle's Point Stairway for a good view of the beaches. Eagle's Point once had twenty-eight trees, but twenty-six of them died of exposure caused by people trampling on the roots. When the stairway was built in 1980, the Park Service raised the ground level to protect the tree roots, and made sure that the railroad ties fitted over them.

☐ This particular kind of stairway is called a *gabion*, French for a certain type of basket used in agriculture. We can see that the side with a basket-weave pattern is actually a retaining wall with risers to hold the wall in. The whole system was built up so that people would have a level tread to go across.

☐ We come back up the stairway and take the path to El Camino del Mar and 32nd Avenue. Houses, yards, and automobiles are in stunning contrast to the sunning seals and earthen footpaths of a moment ago! The Lands End Trail ends here, where the old streetcar route began. The Lake Street bus is two blocks south.

■ Otherwise, we continue on El Camino del Mar toward China Beach, passing McLaren Avenue and turning sharply left to go down elegant Sea Cliff Avenue.

☐ A stone has been placed at the top of the China Beach Stairway to commemorate the Chinese fishermen who used this site. China (formerly James D. Phelan) Beach is well maintained, with lifeguards, a bath house, picnic tables, and benches from which to watch boats. Or to contemplate. . . .

☐ Country and town, nature and people. This side of the city along the ocean, once used for military fortifications by the Spanish and the Americans, is now mostly sand dunes, scrub habitat, and space. The eastern side of San Francisco that was once Yerba Buena, a perfect site for commerce, fishing and shipping, is now a high-density commercial and residential area.

☐ The map of San Francisco shows large expanses of green north and east from the Cliff House on the Great Highway all the way to Hyde Street. It's a wonder to have almost 4000 acres of the city in the Golden Gate National Recreation Area! Let's guard the open space, and encourage the formation of all odd-shaped, uncategorized, informal green areas throughout the city.

☐ The entire Golden Gate National Recreation Area offers an exciting prospect for friends of stairways because new ones are being built. I propose that plaques be placed on each new stairway, giving the date of its construction and the names of the construction crew. We need more *sung* heroes who labor for beauty and nature and man.

☐ Now we can go back to our starting point on foot, or by taking the 38–Geary bus from 33rd Avenue and Geary.

MAP F

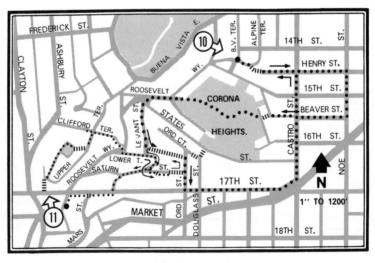

10 ☐ **Between the Houses**
11 ☐ **Bamboo and Lemons**

Between the Houses

Corona Heights, one of San Francisco's forty-three hills, is 510 feet high and very near the city's geographical center. From here, we have easy access to the neighborhoods south of Market Street via Castro and Clayton. This walk, with Walk 11, takes us on both sides of Corona Heights.

A place to enjoy the sun and to picnic, Corona Heights is also the site of the Josephine G. Randall Junior Museum, which has exhibits of geology and Indian artifacts. Classes in natural history and a collection of small animals that can be touched and held make this a popular school trip.

■ We begin at Buena Vista Terrace and Roosevelt Way. Across from 26 Roosevelt is the Henry Stairway, which we descend to Noe Street. On Noe, turn right to Beaver, then another right and up the stairs next to 145 Beaver Way, ending up at the Corona Heights playground.

□ Wending our way to the Junior Museum at 199 Museum Way, we emerge on Fairbanks Street, which is unmarked.

□ Turn left to Levant, then descend the unusual landscaped Vulcan Stairway to a right on Ord Street. (On Walk 11, we go *up* the stairway for a different view.)

□ From Ord we turn left to 17th Street, then left on Castro, then left yet again on Henry Street to the stairway—to find we've trodden a complete circle!

Bamboo and Lemons

If we were to walk from Ocean Beach at the western end of the city and finally arrive at 17th Street and Clayton, we could say we had worked up to it. After the flats, the land begins sloping upward toward 19th Avenue. At about Fourth Avenue and Parnassus, where the University of California is, the altitude is noticeable, as befits the home of the gods.

At 17th and Clayton, we're even higher, entering a relatively unknown area that freeways miss. Because the cut-off streets can entangle cars, but not walkers, uncurious nonresidents don't ordinarily venture here. A thirty-five-year resident of Upper Terrace says that when people realize how difficult it is to maneuver on the narrow street, they usually depart, leaving behind them privacy and quiet.

We can play all kinds of games as we walk here. Even though the advice to "Go West" was meant for distances of 3000 miles, we can adopt the spirit of the explorer. "What's this?" we cry upon seeing some beautiful stairways. Answer: Obviously a natural phenomenon peculiar to this area, formed from the erosion of stones and sand by human feet.

■ We begin. Humming a few bars of "Stairway to the Stars" (at least until the breath gives out), ascend the stairway paralleling an apartment complex near the corner of 17th and Clayton—a very abrupt, ambitious beginning, though the rise extends only from 449 feet to 476.
□ When we reach the top, we are on Upper Terrace.
□ Bear upward to Monument Way, a circular hopscotch form that at one time marked the center of San Francisco. In 1887, Adolph Sutro placed the Olympus Monument here—a sculpture of a Greek goddess. The sculpture has since been damaged, indeed vandalized to near nonexistence. And the 360 degree panorama of the city is partially concealed by overgrowth of shrubbery.
□ We work to catch the view by craning necks this way and that—and every creak and strain is worth it.

■ Next to 480 Monument, the Monument Stairway takes us down to Upper Terrace where we turn left. The houses on this pretty street reinforce the special atmosphere of the area. We follow Upper Terrace to Clifford Terrace where there is a brass plaque dating No. 112 to 1896 and a sundial that states, "Time Takes All but Memories."
□ We return to the corner of Clifford and Upper Terrace and continue east on Clifford. Down six steps, we cross Roosevelt to descend the Roosevelt Way Stairway (which begins at No. 473) to Lower Terrace. We turn left on Lower Terrace and suddenly—this is it—one of

SATURN STREET

the most extraordinary views in San Francisco!

☐ No. 54 Lower Terrace is a stick-style brick red Victorian built in the 1880s that looks as though it escaped from a movie set. The view behind it is unmatched. Someone should do a study of the effect of beautiful views on the beholder. As for us, we are mesmerized.

☐ However, the Lower Terrace Stairway beckons to the south, and we walk on. We descend to Saturn, a grade-separated street.

■ The houses on Saturn are a mixture of materials and styles, of redwood and stucco. They range through an elaborate Queen Anne of the 1890s at No. 133, to flat boxes of the 1950s at Nos. 112 and 118, to bay-windowed, shingled apartments of the 1970s at No. 52. Four sets of stairways lead from the elevated side to the lower half of the street. At the end of Saturn, the Stairway, framed by sweet fennel and overhanging cotoneaster berries, descends to Ord Street.

☐ We walk to the left. Across from No. 7 Ord, we walk up the Vulcan Stairway, a miniature Shangri-La. On one side is a sloping row of remodeled, eclectic, mostly wooden turn-of-the-century cottages. The flexibility of these early houses, whose new, well-designed patios, decks, and skylights extend outdoor living to the interiors, is a marvel. Looking up, we see the back of 54 Lower Terrace, the movie-set house.

☐ A mature date palm imposes itself three-fourths of the way up the Stairway, and the scent of mock-orange blossoms pervades the air. Cypress, eucalyptus, Scotch broom, fuchsia, rhododendron, azaleas, and hydrangeas are in full bloom. Here is a datura, the Australian desert bush that features giant, bell-shaped flowers, and a living fence of bamboo obscures a thriving lemon tree in one of the yards.

☐ Noting the many strange angles to the structures here, we reach Levant. Turning left to Lower Terrace, and continuing to a left turn on Roosevelt, we will find ourselves at our starting point at 17th Street.

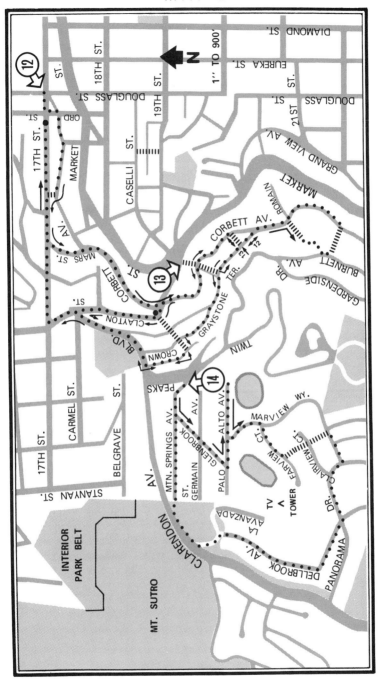

12 □ Theme and Variations
13 □ Half a Cup of Tea
14 □ At Last!

UPPER MARKET TWO

Theme and Variations

The Upper Market neighborhood is vast and full of nooks and crannies. It is becoming more interesting and better known as the gay community extends out from Castro in four directions. New shops are opening on the wide thoroughfare of Market Street and rundown Victorians are being renovated on the smaller streets, which curve beyond our sight into hidden stairways, high walls, and precipitous gardens. The inhabitants show a generally high level of care and attention to the surroundings.

This is a great place for people-watching, especially on Friday and Saturday nights. People are *always* around—window browsing or sitting in open-air restaurants or smoke-filled bars.

This is a long walk. We go from the Upper Market area south as far as Twin Peaks. *(The first part of this long walk, until we reach 17th Street and Douglass, can be followed on Map F. Then we switch to Map G.)*

■ We begin at 15th Street and Castro and continue south on Castro past Beaver, all the while enjoying a view of the Bay and the houses high on a cliff. We go right on States and admire a long-hidden stair/pathway on the north side leading to No. 40. A totem stands there like an eternal spectator. The houses on States are Victorian row houses and cottages embellished with shrubbery, flowers, and Japanese latticework.

☐ Above the empty lots on the right side of the street is the Corona Heights Playground and a footpath to the Josephine Randall Museum. The house at 97 States looks charming enough to move into instantly. Across from No. 184 is the stairway down to Douglass, although this street name cannot be seen.

☐ At the bottom of the stairs, we immediately turn west and walk up the nine steps leading into the Ord Court cul-de-sac, a pleasing detour. We return to Douglass, going south toward 17th Street (here we join Map G) and cross 17th over to Corbett, where we turn right.

☐ We turn left, go uphill on 17th, south to Mars, and follow on to Corbett. The houses here are built close to the street. When we see Market Street below, we realize our elevation. The Mono Street Stairway, whose name is embossed in the sidewalk across from 376 Corbett, is blocked off, but the street continues on the other side of Market.

■ At the corner of Corbett and Clayton, we continue on Corbett past Iron Alley Stairway, which goes down to Market. Across the street is the Corbett School, now used for administrative offices of the school system.

☐ At 555 Corbett, the alley has been blocked by a house below, but that doesn't detract from another superb view. Stop beside 595 Corbett and try to name the hills, which in the distance appear barren. Corona Heights is one. Is it possible we've come such a distance?

☐ We cross the street and go up Copper Stairway, which deadends at Graystone, which we follow southeast back to Corbett. We pass Glendale Stairway on our way to the Corbett Stairs across the street at Rooftop School. An overpass across the street at the corner of Romain continues to the other side of Market.

■ We go up the stairs of Rooftop School, enter the schoolyard, jog left, and go upstairs to Burnett.

☐ A few feet away, next to 449 Burnett, is the Dixie Stairway, which we descend to Corbett, next to No. 801. We turn left and then bear left to Graystone. Be careful here! Corbett and Graystone form a V. Keep to the left or you'll retrace your steps.

☐ At Pemberton, we ascend the stairway to Crown Terrace.

☐ We turn north to Twin Peaks Boulevard, down to 17th Street, turn right to Castro, and north to 15th. For the hungry, there are delicatessens in the immediate vicinity, or continue on to Castro and 18th for a larger selection of restaurants.

PEMBERTON PLACE

Half a Cup of Tea

In the middle of the city is an outcropping of Franciscan Formation, rock composed of chert, shale, volcanic rock, and graywacke sandstone. Man insisted upon streets, and the rock, not taking kindly to grid plan, said, "Yes, but only so far." Thus began a contest of angle versus contour.

One outcome of this encounter is an inner area blocked to vehicles—pedestrians only. Beguiling stairways here lead into other stairways. The short streets, sometimes unfinished, make it in many ways comparable to the eastern side of the city. But the hills are higher than Telegraph and Russian Hill, and the area was developed much later than those closer to water.

The White Rabbit in *Alice in Wonderland* wanted only a half-cup of tea. Well, this walk is like that. You may take either half (11 and 13), or a whole, and be astounded at how sides of the city curve into each other to make a bridge across the length and breadth of San Francisco.

■ We begin at Market and Iron Alley Stairway, just southeast of Clayton. Go up wooden stairs to Graystone, turn left to Copper Alley Stairway and descend to Corbett, where we turn left to continue to Clayton. We go forward, north to Twin Peaks Boulevard near Carmel, and turn left, reversing our direction, going southwest to Crown Terrace.

☐ This charming street is part of the section known in the 1930s as Little Italy—the Bank of Italy, now Bank of America, held many of the neighborhood's mortgages (and many of them were foreclosed during the Depression).

☐ We walk the length of Crown Terrace for the sheer pleasure of it, then come back to 98 Crown, where we descend the majestic Pemberton Stairway. The architectural variety here is delightful and views between the houses abound.

■ As the stairway becomes wider, so widens a sense of expansiveness and well-being. It is presumptuous to expect this to be the norm for stairways; think of those less well-planned.

☐ The residents on Pemberton lovingly maintain these stairs. They have landscaped the textures, masses, and colors of the shrubs and flowers to complement and contrast in both dramatic and natural patterns.

■ Each time I take this walk, I imagine myself in fine velvet and lace, descending, slowly and in measured cadence, the ballroom staircase in *War and Peace,* to be swept into a sea of waltzers. But awake! A few more steps, a few more minutes, and we are near our starting point, still wearing jeans and hiking boots.

At Last!

New York has its Statue of Liberty, Chicago has its Wrigley Building, Houston its Astrodome, Seattle the Space Needle, and San Francisco—its television tower on Mt. Sutro. We have seen it from different angles and from different locations throughout the city. Now we see this Sutro tower closeup and in full scale; we feel we are in the presence of the Golem, the frightening, fascinating mechanical creature from Yiddish folklore, the prototype of Frankenstein.

■ We begin our outing at Twin Peaks Boulevard and Mountain Spring. Walk up Mountain Spring past No. 30, a used-brick structure with round arches that resembles a winery and that looks out to a splendid view from the back. We cross the street to walk southwest on Glenbrook.

☐ Immediately ahead of us, across Palo Alto Avenue, is the television tower. So this is the reason for faulty television reception, for radio interference, for all kinds of electronic hum and buzz! Let's put some distance between us!

☐ We're above the fog line, with one of those seductive views toward the north that residents here say is their reward for the depression they suffer from continual summer fog.

☐ We turn left on Palo Alto, walk to the end of the street, and experience a surreal view. An undulating, concealing swath of fog has divided our side of the landscape from the East Bay. Alcatraz is almost hidden behind a scrim curtain. We gape, with the soundless terror we feel from a rapid elevator descent. How many steps to the chasm? Are we on the edge of the earth?

■ The house at 100 Palo Alto was the residence of Elmer Robinson, mayor of San Francisco from 1948 to 1956. The Twin Peaks Reservoir, just to our right, is used to charge the large blue red-topped hydrants that are part of the Fire Department's auxiliary water supply.

☐ Backtrack on Palo Alto to go left on Marview Way and right on Farview Court. Tract houses here have telescoped backyards which abut the Sutro tower.

☐ Next to 50 Farview is the Fridela Lane Stairway. It has fewer than sixty steps, but the high risers and steep angle remind us of the stairs of the Mayan Pyramids.

☐ We descend another forty steps to cross Clairview Court, and down to Marview, where we turn right, again right on Panorama, and yet another right on Dellbrook. We walk on the even-numbered side of Dellbrook that backs into Mt. Sutro.

☐ From Dellbrook we turn left onto Clarendon, and follow it northeast to Mountain Spring Avenue. Continue on Mountain Spring and here we are back at our beginning.

MAP H

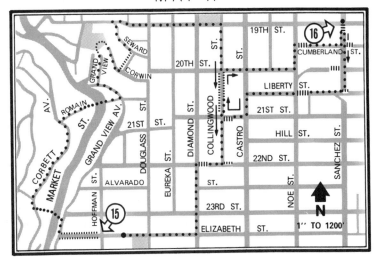

15 ☐ Forbidden Footpaths
16 ☐ If It Feels Like a Dance, It's a Good Walk

Forbidden Footpaths

Eureka Valley encompasses the area below the southern slope of Twin Peaks. It is wedged between Diamond Heights, Noe Valley, and Upper Market.

Eureka Valley's Castro Street is the hub of the gay community, an important sociological and political force in San Francisco since 1970.

In 1977, Harvey Milk became the first admittedly gay member of the San Francisco Board of Supervisors. After his and Mayor George Moscone's murder in 1978 by a deranged former supervisor, Milk was replaced by another gay, Harry Britt, who has since been re-elected. The gay movement's militancy has brought about reforms in police hiring policies, as well as in practices of harassment in the workplace.

Castro Street supports a variety of boutiques and stores (for coffee beans, flowers, antiques, and other specialties), many restaurants and bars, and the Castro Theatre, a 1923 movie palace that has Landmark status.

On Halloween, Castro Street bank tellers, clerks, and business people don makeup. Later, the street between Market and 18th is blocked to auto traffic while *everybody* is out in costume—elaborate, outrageous, and colorful. No celebration anywhere else is quite like it.

The gay influence shows in the brisk renovation of homes and gardens. This is one area where taxis are always in use by the affluent, and where many people carry bouquets—even on Monday morning.

■ On this walk, an eloquent cadence of steps, alleyways, views, and overpasses is repeated over and over again. We begin at Elizabeth and Hoffman Streets and walk west on the north side of the Elizabeth sidewalk steps to Grand View Avenue. We cross Grand View, bear right to the circular overpass over Market, and continue onto the path to Corbett. We turn right onto Corbett and follow it to Romain where we turn right.

☐ Pastel houses and a *big* view characterize this street.

☐ From this cul-de-sac, we continue over the walkway above Market Street. Romain begins again at Market, and we curve left on Grand View and turn right to Grand View Terrace. Next to No. 59 is a steep, treacherous footpath down to Corwin. It would be a civilized gesture by the city and the Pacific Gas and Electric Company to convert these easements into walkable footpaths with plantings on both sides!

☐ On Grand View Terrace, we follow the U-shaped Kite Hill footpath from west to east. Kite Hill will be developed as a hilltop park. Naturally, it is enveloped by views.

■ No. 185 Corwin, a two-story beige stucco apartment building with brown trim, surprises us by being where we expect more unoccupied

ELIZABETH STREET

ground. The view in front of No. 185 looks straight down the spine of Market Street to the Ferry Building. The driveway to the left of 66 Corwin is part of Acme Alley. Cobblestones peeking from the partial cover of cement add the contrasting flavor of age to the adjoining Seward Park Playground.

☐ We walk through the Park and turn left onto Seward, then right to 19th Street and within a few blocks right onto Collingwood, where we begin a strenuous climb up a thirty degree slope on our right. The street used to be known, quite aptly, as Goat Hill.

☐ At 20th Street, use the Collingwood sidewalk stairway and then the grooved sidewalk. At 21st the remnants of the original level of the street are visible, as well as the filled portions extending to the 400 block of Collingwood. The houses below the street level were built before the street was "improved."

☐ Next to 433 Collingwood is Castro, here the driveway and right of way, not yet approved by the city, for the houses fronting the upper level of Castro Street.

☐ On the west side of Collingwood is No. 480, a house built by a German mason in 1932 of cobblestones from the dismantled Castro cable car line. Collingwood is only five blocks long, ending in a cul-de-sac at 22nd Street with stairways going east and west.

☐ We take the west stairway, the one on the right, lined on either side with eucalyptus and a huge palm tree, to Diamond. Our elevation and distance give the tourists we see on Twin Peaks the dimensions of Jonathan Swift's Lilliputians, ten thousand of whom could stand on the body of normal-sized Gulliver.

☐ We turn left on Diamond, then right on Elizabeth, back to the beginning.

If It Feels Like a Dance,
It's a Good Walk

There's more to a good walk than fresh air and length. What about the shape of it?

Do walks really have shapes?

Indeed they do.

Why are some walks just right, others nondescript? It's the shape, of course. If we draw the outline of a walk, and if it flows like a dance and feels like a dance, it's a good walk.

To illustrate: Our first walk on Dolores Heights looked like this:

Our final version looked like this:

See what shapes mean?

In Dolores Heights, we can't see the shape of the land for the many, many stairways, but we can feel it. A walk in Dolores Heights is sheer choreography!

■ We begin at 19th and Sanchez and, breathing deeply, ascend the stairway. At the top are four aged cypresses overgrown with English ivy.

☐ We walk on the east side of Sanchez and continue south. At one time, Sanchez had brick paving, but it was too slick and had to be covered with asphalt. One of the houses on this block is supposed to have a capped spring underneath.

☐ Passing Cumberland, notice the extraordinarily beautiful pine at the corner. (I might as well confess now that Cumberland and Sanchez is one of my favorite corners in San Francisco.)

☐ Continue to Liberty and turn right. This area is a former goat farm. The seven brick houses at 450 Liberty, with a common entrance and parking area, are a planned community built in 1966. They enjoy a clear view to the east overlooking Dolores Park. They also enjoy a stairway at the end of the common walk descending to 20th Street.

SANCHEZ STREET

■ Continue to the Liberty Stairway and descend to Noe Street. The four white stucco houses by the stairway are a testimonial to the Art Deco architecture of the 1930s. From here, we can see almost all of the television tower on Mount Sutro.

☐ Walking on the south side of Liberty at Noe, we see a scooped skyline to the north. Corona Hill and former St. Joseph's Hospital (now being made into condominiums) are to the west; the highrises in the financial district are toward the east. There is a dense plane tree in front of 521 Liberty and a mature hibiscus across the street.

☐ As we approach Castro, our view of the Sutro tower has been reduced to the top third. Queen Anne row houses are on the west side of the 700 block of Castro.

■ We turn left onto Castro heading south to 21st. Turn right and walk on the south side. From Castro to Diamond, 21st Street used to be extremely steep. In 1924, the city modified this by lowering the grade on one side and filling in the street on the other. These structural changes are still evident in the low foundations of the pre-1924 houses and in the non-useable garages. The houses with higher foundations were built after 1924.

☐ At Collingwood, turn right and go down the grooved sidewalk stairs that begin at No. 322, to 20th Street. In 1924, Collingwood was also "improved" from 20th to 22nd Street. Now a rat's nest of overhead wires snarls the 300 block.

☐ Still in sight of three-quarters of the ubiquitous Sutro tower, we turn right on 20th and go past Castro to Noe, where we turn left and walk on the east side of the street to the stairway going up to Cumberland.

☐ The cul-de-sac entrance at the top of the stairs begins a pleasant walk alongside trees and houses. The air bears the scent of pittosporum and solanum. In the front yard at 338 Cumberland, honeydew melons are growing in a wire cage. We continue to Sanchez.

☐ We turn left and descend the Sanchez Stairway to our beginning. Eating places and stairway extensions surround us to the south and west.

MAP I

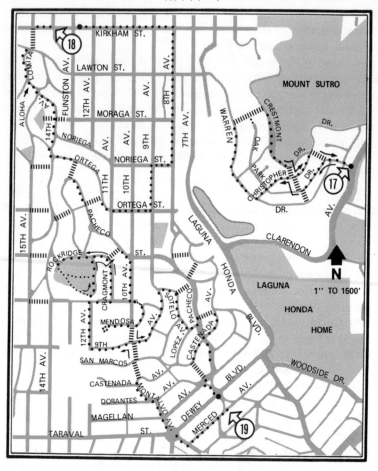

17 ☐ Grading and Sliding
18 ☐ Lead Thread on a Sugar Bag
19 ☐ Marienbad in San Francisco

Grading and Sliding

Franciscan rock, on which much of Forest Knolls is built, doesn't settle. Instead of forming neat layers, it makes helter-skelter angles. After a landslide here in 1966, a building moratorium was declared for ten years. We recently saw a newly built house on Warren Street that slid down the slope before the owner had a chance to move in. Engineering and contracting reports are required by the city before building permits are issued, but as of now geologists are not required to report directly to the Planning Department before new developments are built. Forest Knolls presents an excellent illustration of the problems and dangers of grading hills composed of Franciscan rock.

■ We begin our walk at Clarendon and Oak Park, which we follow as it curves to the southwest. Between No. 301 and No. 291 Oak Park is the Blairwood Lane Stairway. We walk up half-way to Christopher. The plantings across the street are beautifully terraced with pines, eucalyptus, ice plants, century plants, and marguerites. To the right, the fog hangs in the eucalyptus trees on Mt. Sutro.

☐ We turn left on Christopher and follow it to Warren, take a right, and continue on Warren to the Oakhurst Stairway next to No. 398.

☐ The word "hurst," which is so often found attached to English village names, means "wood"—Oakhurst is aptly named. Skunks and other small mammals live in this area, at one time Adolph Sutro's hunting grounds. In his prime, Sutro owned one-twelfth of San Francisco, and planted more than half a million trees on his property. Sutro is a favorite pioneer. With each walk, he becomes more dear as we realize how much he enriched us all by foresting the hills.

■ Well, here we go, up Oakhurst Stairway. We feel we are trudging through the opening scene of Charlie Chaplin's *The Gold Rush*. Though there is no snow, there are instead eucalyptus, bottlebrush, daisies, weeds, weeds, weeds, ice plants, mallow, and the ocean, as far as the eye can see.

☐ The climb is steep in this eucalyptus forest. Half-way up the zigzag stairway, we sit on the steps to admire an extraordinary wide-angle view. An ocean liner—ever romantic—travels east. St. Anne's Church on Judah and Funston is visible through the fog. So is the Public Health Hospital at 15th Avenue and Lake Street

☐ But there are more steps to walk. Finally we are at Oak Park, where a little walkway goes into a cul-de-sac. Back to the stairs, we continue to Crestmont Drive. We turn right. The foliage here is so thick that many wild creatures must be enjoying concealment as we pass by. Across the street, a huge retaining wall delineates Sutro Woods development.

☐ At Crestmont and Devonshire, the fog is gaining on us rapidly. Each house on Crestmont has a garden reached via stairs. Between Nos. 95 and 101, by a white fire hydrant, is the Blairwood Lane Stairway.

■ We descend to Christopher and turn left. At 191 Christopher, we find a walkway-stairway that goes down to Oak Park. This has no sign, but one map lists it as Glenhaven Lane. This stairway takes us back to our starting point.

☐ Want a shorter alternative to this walk? Begin at Seventh Avenue and Lawton in the Sunset District. Proceed east on Lawton to Warren. Go south to Oakhurst Lane Stairway and climb up to Crestmont Drive. Turn right, continue past Devonshire Way to Blairwood Lane Stairway and walk down to Warren.

18

GOLDEN GATE HEIGHTS

Lead Thread on a Sugar Bag

The vast tract of land known as the Sunset District sprawls from Sloat Boulevard to Golden Gate Park and from Stanyan Street to the Pacific Ocean. At one time, it was all sand dunes, and even now the Great Highway is sometimes silted over from the frequent winds that sweep off the beach. The Sunset gets more wind and fog than any other place in the city, but the people who live there claim to love it for the ocean view, the magnificent sunsets, and (when it's not fog-bound) the clear, clean air.

After the establishment of Golden Gate Park in 1870, the Sunset was sparsely settled by pioneers, then settled a bit more after the earthquake of 1906. Some of the squatters' cottages along the Great Highway have been in use since then. The H Street (now Lincoln Avenue) railway brought more settlers after World War I. Along about this time, the named streets of the Sunset were laid out in an alphabetical grid pattern, from Irving (Judah, Kirkham, Lawton, etc.) on southward. The *numbered avenues* that cross the streets align with their likes across Golden Gate Park, which intercepts them.

After World War II, Henry Doelger and other contractors built the mass-produced designs that are a district trademark. Now the Sunset seems to be just about filled up with a varied population consisting of middle class families of many different racial origins. The 1980 Census indicates that the Sunset has the largest proportion of people over sixty in any San Francisco neighborhood. The University of California Medical School on Parnassus Avenue accounts for the large transient student population.

One of the Sunset's many subdivisions is Golden Gate Heights. A walk here is reminiscent of a sugar-sack thread. To open sewn sugar sacks with one motion, one found and pulled the beginning loop thread that automatically unwound the other loops. Voila! The bag was open. People who couldn't find that lead thread had to use scissors to snip off individual loops, which was neither neat nor convenient.

Until I found the lead stairway in the Golden Gate Heights neighborhood, I was zizagging and retracing my steps over and over. The present ramble is a natural refinement of all the misguided turns I took to find that lead stairway.

■ We begin on Kirkham at 14th Avenue, walking west on the south side to the stairway next to 1502 15th Avenue.

□ We take the 160 steps upward at a slow pace to savor the view from each landing. At the fourth landing, we can see the twin spires of St. Ignatius Church to the northeast. At the fifth landing, toward the right, St. Anne's of the Sunset Church is in view, and behind it, toward the right, the Byzantine dome of Temple Emanu-el. Before us toward the north are the Marin hills and the red lead towers of the Golden Gate Bridge, half covered by the scalloped tops of the trees in Golden Gate Park. At Lawton and Lomita, we come at last to the top of the stairway.

□ Walk slightly right and straight ahead on Lomita, and continue to the intersection of Aloha. We bear left on Aloha (tricky because the street signs seem mis-angled). At the intersection of Aloha, 15th Avenue, and 14th Avenue, we cross the street and bear left onto 14th, walking on the lower separation—the one with the sidewalk. A high retaining wall is on the other side. (Regardless of an exterior lack of logic, these streets really do flow in an organic pattern.)

■ At Moraga, a divided stairway descends to Funston and ascends to the top of Grand View Park, a superb place to watch the sunset.

□ Difficult as it is to ignore these stairways, we continue on 14th past Noriega. The corner is an open hillside of Franciscan rock—beautiful in its contorted way and dangerous in its instability. A favorite house is 601 Ortega, which is built up dramatically on the Franciscan outcropping.

□ The Cascade Stairway is on the east side of No. 601. We walk up about 130 gradual steps to Pacheco. Carl E. Larsen, a Danish restaurateur, loved this area. By the time of his death in 1924 at age 84, he had given the city six acres of land in the Golden Gate Heights, including the Sunset Heights Park (recently renamed Golden Gate Heights Park) featured in Walk 19.

☐ We make a left turn to Pacheco and see the Mt. Davidson cross, Twin Peaks, and the Mt. Sutro television tower. We continue on Pacheco to Aerial Stairway on the left. As we walk down 114 steps, we note the homes on stilts near Mt. Sutro.

☐ We turn right on Ortega, past a cobblestoned driveway and a beautiful series of brick and rail stairs at No. 445. From the corner of 11th Avenue and Ortega, we continue east downhill on Ortega. No. 239 is a Craftsman style bungalow with an owl in the gable and a stone foundation. One block farther on we make a left turn onto Ninth Avenue, and a right on Noriega to Eighth.

■ We can see the deep canyon going down to Seventh Avenue from the fenced area on the east side of the street. The unused Laguna Honda reservoir is to our left at the bottom of the hill.

☐ Turn left on Eighth Avenue and walk on the west side of the street to get a better view of the row houses across from us in the 1700 block. Their pastel colors are graduated in intensity and the total combination is pleasing. The deep canyon is fenced on Moraga and Eighth.

☐ A brick sign announces the entrance to Windsor Terrace, built in 1913, with attractive large detached homes and pleasing trees.

☐ We continue north on Eighth to Kirkham and left to 14th Avenue, our beginning.

☐ We could continue north to Judah and Irving streets. The latter is a personal, friendly, older neighborhood shopping center, with many family-owned stores. In addition, along Ninth Avenue from Judah to Lincoln are rows of specialty shops, restaurants, bookstores, a shoe shop, a garage painted with murals of Swiss scenes, cafe espresso retreats, and a natural-food store.

19

FOREST HILL

Marienbad in San Francisco

It's not the longest stairway in the city. The Filbert and Vallejo Stairways are longer. Nor the steepest. Oakhurst is steeper. Vulcan and Harry are more charming, and Pemberton more personal.

However, the grand Pacheco Stairway is by far the most elegant in San Francisco. An urn of flowers twenty feet in diameter introduces this long staircase placed amidst forest and lawns. The stairs themselves—eighteen-and-a-half feet wide with balustrades, columns, and a pattern of stones repeating into the distance, lend the setting a dreamlike quality (directed by Alain Resnais): were we or were we not at Marienbad last year? Did we or did we not traverse Pacheco Stairway long, long ago?

Our rococo walk of curves and curlicues reiterates the innate elegance of Pacheco Stairway in its Forest Hill setting.

Forest Hill was originally part of the 4000-acre Rancho San Miguel, granted in 1843 to José de Jesus Noe, the last Mexican *alcalde* of San Francisco. After California became independent, the eleven ranchos that comprised the town were subdivided. In 1880, Adolph Sutro bought 1100 acres of Noe's rancho; Crocker's estate bought the rest.

Forest Hill was one of the earliest tract developments in the western part of the city and was planned to complement the Twin Peaks Tunnel, which was to provide easy transportation to downtown.

In 1912, the Newell-Murdoch Company, a real estate firm, began subdividing the Forest Hill tract, cutting down much of what had been extremely dense forest planted by Adolph Sutro and his troops of eager school children. Difficult engineering and construction problems were solved in a most esthetic manner by Mark Daniels, the landscape engineer, who deserves a plaque commending his designs of curving streets, generous stairways, ornamental urns, concrete benches, balustrades, parks, and terraces.

Construction of the first house, at 266 Pacheco, was begun in 1913. By the time the Tunnel was completed in 1917, twenty homes had been built. In 1918, the first streetcar went through the Tunnel and the Forest Hill Association was formed. It imposed home-building restrictions, some of which are still in effect, such as a minimum 1500-square-foot interior and a nineteen-foot setback from the sidewalk.

The streets and stairways, delightful and unconforming, do not meet city specifications, so the Association has been responsible for maintenance. After years of controversy and court action, San Francisco accepted Forest Hill in 1978 as its responsibility but did not begin work on the deteriorating streets until 1982.

In the meantime, the "Grand" stairway has no official name, so we call it Pacheco, linking it to an important adjacent street.

■ We begin at the intersection of Merced and Pacheco to view the fine planning north into Forest Hill and south into the Edgehill neighborhood along the axis of the Pacheco Stairway.

PACHECO STREET

☐ We walk southwest on Merced to Kensington where we turn right, cross Dewey Street, and continue to Magellan, detouring right to No. 381, the Forest Hill Clubhouse. Designed by Bernard Maybeck, an architect associated with the Craftsman school of architecture in California, the Clubhouse is characteristic of Maybeck's work in the use of natural redwood for beams and walls, pitched roofs, and large-paned windows that allow light and views to come inside.

☐ Maybeck donated the Clubhouse plans to his friend, Edwin Young, a Forest Hill resident, and club members donated their labor. The original cost of this inviting 1919 structure, used for weddings and receptions as well as club events, was $10,000.

☐ Forest Hill has the greatest concentration of Maybeck homes in San Francisco. We will pass most of them on our walk.

■ Turn back from Magellan to Montalvo and go north. We pass a Rapunzel-towered house on our left, wondering how much more spinning of gold is left to do, and arrive at 376 Castenada, with its several slate gables and three greenhouses. The original owner was an orchid fancier whose collection is in the Conservatory in Golden Gate Park.

☐ Next door, take the stairway that ascends two levels across San Marcos, emerging onto Ninth Avenue. We turn left, and walk west to Twelfth Avenue, then right toward Golden Gate Heights Park (once Sunset Heights Park).

☐ Now we are in the Sunset Heights neighborhood. The houses are smaller, detached, and more uniform in style, dating from the 1950s and 1960s. There *is* a park up there, but we will have to walk around the block to reach it. From Twelfth Avenue we turn right on Quintara, then left on Cragmont, bending to the left on Rockridge, which circles to a park entrance. We walk eastward on the soft footpath in Golden Gate Heights Park, one of the loveliest neighborhood parks in San Francisco. With almost five acres, this park offers opportunities for active sports, visiting, picnicking, and botanizing. Trees and shrubs are mature; multihued fungi proliferate after rain.

☐ This park is part of 250,000 square feet of land bequeathed to San Francisco by Carl Larsen in the 1920s. Larsen had used it as his chicken ranch and its fresh eggs received top billing on his Tivoli Cafe menu. On Easter Sunday, city children participated in a joyous egg hunt that became a San Francisco tradition.

■ A choice of footpaths through the park brings us down to Twelfth Avenue. We amble along Quintara to Cragmont Avenue, turn left, and follow the street to the Oriole Stairway, which we descend to Pacheco. There we have an extensive vista that includes Twin Peaks and the Mt. Davidson cross.

☐ We turn right on Pacheco, right on Tenth Avenue to Quintara, and walk to the left to the end of the street. But behold! It's not the end by any means.

☐ The prospect of walking on a footpath through an open gateway up the S-curve of Mendosa, a densely foliaged street with concealed tucked-in houses all around, is certainly charming.

☐ We follow Mendosa past Tenth and past Gateview Court to its natural cul-de-sac. The extension of Mendosa, rocky and hilly before the advent of the bulldozer, is now almost completely developed.

☐ The hemispherical view from the point is a San Francisco special. A bench was recently placed here to enhance the viewing and the sand is now covered and held by moss campion and daisies. Atmospheric conditions over the ocean radiate a translucent chiaroscuro over the city's hilltops and rooftops, and over the clouds themselves.

☐ Moving away from this scene is one of the most difficult parts of our walk, but there is humorous contrast at the other end of the Mendosa cul-de-sac near the water-pumping station: two houses built in the shape of ships. Though there are several ship-shaped houses in San Francisco, these two are the most shiplike, and fine planning shows in their location at the edge of a precipice where the captain might take a reading from the upper deck with the Pacific Ocean practically in his front yard.

■ Back down the stairway next to 91 Mendosa, we are now on upper Ninth Avenue, and turn left. No. 2230 was originally a Maybeck, but later renovations make it unrecognizable.

☐ We walk a block and turn right onto Sotelo. No. 51 is a Maybeck built in 1914 for his friend E. H. Young. A curved wood design accents the Juliette balcony.

☐ We continue to No.1 Sotelo, and bear left into Lopez, again left onto Pacheco, descending the stairway on the right next to No. 334.

☐ Along the stairway on our left is 140 Castenada, a Maybeck built in 1924. The new owner, entranced with Maybeck's design, used the original construction style to very good effect when he refurbished. Approach the front for a closer look at the carving of grape vines, a symbol of fecundity, along the eaves.

☐ Turn right on Castenada and walk toward the stairway next to No. 245. A large Maybeck with a carriage house, built in 1918, is across the street at No. 270.

☐ As we descend the grand Pacheco Stairway back to the street, think of Jerry Healy. As first superintendent gardener of the tract, he was called "Mayor of Forest Hill." It was Healy who planted geraniums and marguerites so that the area was a mass of red and white colors.

☐ And here we are at our beginning, Pacheco and Merced. Were we walking through *Last Year at Mariendbad*? No, it is this year in San Francisco, where vistas can be infinite and universal.

MAP J

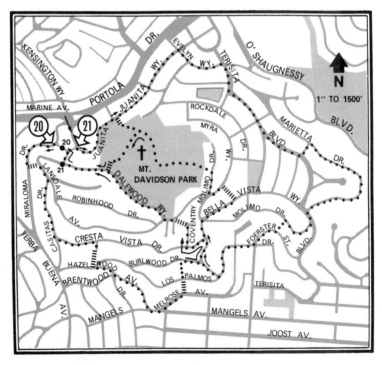

20 ☐ Now You See It, Now You Don't
21 ☐ The Walk of Left-Sided Views

MIRALOMA PARK

Now You See It,
Now You Don't

The area surrounding Mt. Davidson, which at 927 feet is the highest hill in San Francisco, is an interesting mixture of many subneighborhood sections. We traverse several: Sherwood Forest (there's a Robin Hood Drive here), Westwood Highlands, and Miraloma Park. From the small houses in the eastern Miraloma section, the homes gradually become larger west and north toward Mt. Davidson.

Generically, this part of the enormous area west of Twin Peaks is the Mt. Davidson/Miraloma Park neighborhood. Our walk is a field trip in applied sociology, architecture, and real estate theory.

■ We begin at Juanita Alley and Miraloma Drive and walk south on the west side of Miraloma, a street that sports large unattached homes, long wide alleyways, lots of views, and many trees. Next to No. 95 is the narrow Bengal Stairway with wooden risers, concrete steps, and cobblestone steps farther on.

☐ We walk on the stairway to Lansdale and turn right to lower Casitas. Our view to the north encompasses the heights of Forest Hill, Edgehill, and to the south the San Bruno Mountains with homes terraced in figure-eight patterns.

☐ We continue south, then turn left on Cresta Vista. Next to No. 96 is the Globe Alley Stairway, a combination easement and stairway, which we follow down to Hazelwood Avenue, ending where Los Palmos, Brentwood, and Hazelwood come together.

☐ We walk in a southeasterly direction to Brentwood, which seems to end at Melrose and Mangels. How many streets can converge on the head of a junction?

☐ Walk on Melrose. Between Nos. 480 and 500 is the Lulu Alley Stairway which we follow up to Los Palmos, at which point Lulu becomes a steep thirty-degree-grade footpath among the eucalyptus. (When it's muddy, walk on Los Palmos to Bella Vista.) Follow Lulu Alley to Burlwood, turning right, and then left on Bella Vista, and left on Cresta Vista. Spanish words like "cresta" (hillside) and "vista" (view) can only lead us upward.

☐ Turning right on Coventry to Myra Way, we discover a walkway all but hidden next to No. 95. When Myra Street becomes visible, we bear left to Dalewood Way, which skirts Mt. Davidson. At the bottom of the hill, we bear right on Lansdale, where we may see a hydrangea bush at No. 4 with twenty-one-inch flowers! What better testimonial to fog?

■ We turn left on Juanita to Miraloma, to our starting point.

☐ Just for fun, go one block farther northeast to Marne Avenue for an extraordinary sight. We look east and see the Mt. Davidson Cross on the righthand side above a convex of Monterey pine and cypress that borders the sky. As we walk in any direction, the cross seems to shift like the moon. Now you see it—now you don't.

21

MOUNT DAVIDSON

The Walk of Left-Sided Views

Binoculars really ought to be taken on this walk.

Although Mt. Davidson is the highest hill in San Francisco, it is so thickly covered with eucalyptus and pine trees that it does not afford a view. We can see out toward the southeast only from the chaparral side of the mountain. However, some of the most inspiring views in the entire city may be seen from streets like Marietta Drive and Bella Vista, without the twenty-minute wait that is often obligatory from the top of Telegraph Hill.

■ We begin at Marne and Juanita Way and walk east on Juanita. Across from No. 284 is a stairway into the park which might turn out to be our exit of choice.

☐ As we walk along the side of the hill, layered striations of rock are visible. At Evelyn, we see the Cross in profile and follow it as we turn right and then right again on Teresita Boulevard. We continue past the water reservoir at Agua (where else?) in a southeasterly direction. New vistas emerge every few feet on our left.

☐ We pass Reposa and turn left on Arroyo and right on Marietta Drive, and walk on the upper sidewalk. Farther along the 300 block, a sixteenth-century Italian Renaissance landscape of church steeples among rocky canyons gradually unfolds.

■ Glad to have binoculars along? As we face east and turn south in front of 396 Marietta we see: the crane at the Hunters Point Naval Shipyard, Bayview, McLaren Park with its blue water tower, Candlestick Park, the crisscross pattern of houses in the southern hills, and San Bruno Mountain, bristling with television and radio antennas. Reversing our optical direction, we pinpoint some buildings at middle distance: St. John's School on Chenery, a beige building with a bell tower, Simpson Bible College on Silver Avenue, a red brick structure with a balanced row of windows, and the Jewish Home for the Aged on Silver Avenue, also of red brick.

☐ Southbound traffic on Highway 280, the freeway nearest us, is hidden from view by the Glen Park BART station on Bosworth Street. Below, O'Shaughnessy Boulevard outlines the contours of the Miraloma neighborhood and separates it from Glen Canyon Park and Diamond Heights.

☐ We curve in a southwest direction to follow Molimo Drive. Next to 95 Molimo is Gatun Alley, an "anonymous" walking easement which we follow down to Foerster, where we turn right on Los Palmos and again right on Bella Vista.

☐ The corner of Burlwood and the undeveloped side of Bella Vista is a sanctuary where we can catch the performance of white crown sparrows and other birds. Bella Vista at Molimo Drive is an outstanding viewing station.

■ We continue on Bella Vista and walk up the Dorcas Stairway next to No. 222, bordering the Miraloma School. The plantings around it have been the self-imposed and lovingly executed task of a neighboring resident.

☐ At Myra Way, the stairs end. We can end the walk here and can hop on a No. 34 bus—but a superspectacular view farther on would be missed.

☐ We turn left and then right on Molimo Drive. Molimo Drive becomes a cul-de-sac, but before that there is a way out—a footpath that goes up Mt. Davidson, upon which we proceed slowly, not only because it's a significant climb, but because of the wonder of this walk. As we go upward, we can pivot around to view the circumference of San Francisco!

☐ We walk to the right of the Cross and take the footpath down a nature trail among eucalyptus and pine.

☐ This part of the walk is free-form, with a choice of several stairways of stone and moss to get to the beginning. Whichever footpath will be fine.

☐ We come out on Dalewood Way and follow it to Marne and Juanita (or directly onto Juanita) where we began.

MAP K

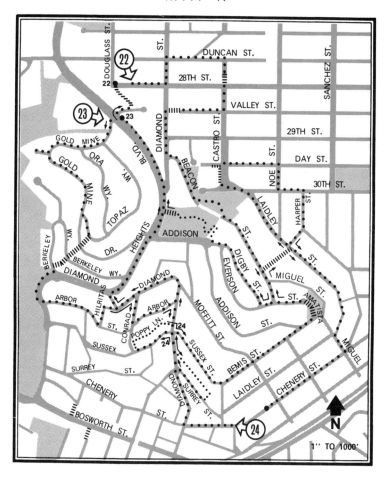

22 □ Diamonds, Diamonds Everywhere
23 □ Rocks, Minerals, and H₂O
24 □ A Twitton and a Bucket for Blackberries

Diamonds, Diamonds Everywhere

Geographically, we are near the middle of the city, on a walk that designs itself. We follow its lead along streets that connect and disconnect strangely, weaving in and out of two neighborhoods, woofing and warping by a miraculous circular route back to our starting point. Cliffs and steep grades may halt vehicles, but a walker goes through.

After World War II, Diamond Heights was one of the first areas in the country to be a federally assisted redevelopment project. Housing ranges widely, from low-cost to custom-built homes. I lament the scanty imagination of its developers in designating names—Diamond Heights, Diamond Street, Diamond Heights Boulevard. . . .

■ We begin our walk at Douglass and 28th Streets. Diamond Heights Village, an apartment complex, is built around the dead-end curve at 28th Street. We amble down the driveway and are startled to discover an outdoor swimming pool for residents. Back on 28th Street, we see Corona Heights (elevation 510 feet) and former St. Joseph's Hospital on Buena Vista toward the north. We walk east on 28th, descending the hill into Noe Valley. The East Bay unfurls before us, perhaps with a pall of smog, perhaps with a veil of fog.

☐ We turn left, walking north on Diamond, and turn right to Duncan. The house at the northeast corner of Newburgh and Duncan has a circular outdoor staircase that goes up to a new sundeck. Across the street on Duncan, high on the hill, are detached houses accessible from long steep stairways. The front gardens are "natural" and straggly.

☐ We continue climbing Duncan, which has no sidewalk on either side. The Bureau of Engineers lists part of Duncan between Sanchez and Noe as a fifty-percent grade, closed to vehicular traffic.

☐ Now we begin to see rooftops of a whole side of the city. The houses around Twin Peaks look like toy blocks.

☐ Turning right on Castro, we see Fairmount Hill Apartments on the southeast side at Duncan Street, houseless hills on the right.

☐ Castro Street has two sections interrupted by stairways and another isolated two-block section in Glen Park. We are now at one end that is blocked off. Here we descend the Castro Stairway to 28th Street.

☐ At 2123 Castro, a fence beautifully follows the slope of the hill, and at 2142, a redwood tree grows.

■ We turn right on Valley Street. The sidewalk stairway at 538 Valley parallels the houses on the upper grade separation and ascends to the end of the street. At the tip of the Valley cul-de-sac another flight of 69 steps goes up to Diamond Street.

□ We turn left on Diamond Street. No. 1700 Diamond is a delightful low-roofed structure, almost hidden by a bamboo fence and four pine trees. Brick stairs curve to the entrance.

□ The area between Diamond, Valley, and 29th Streets is a haven for wildlife. Seeds scattered by wind and birds have resulted in clumps of fennel and poppies. On the left side of the street are four redwood houses, each set a little lower than its neighbor, and all with remarkable views.

□ People do find shortcuts. Here's a worn footpath through a vacant lot to Diamond Heights Boulevard. But we turn left on Beacon and follow an exquisite curve in a southeast direction. There are steep empty lots and no sidewalks on the east side. The view won't be mentioned any more because it's everywhere. Many of the homes here were built in the 1960s by Joseph Eichler, one of the pioneers of architect-designed tract homes in the Bay Area. The graceless townhouses across the street provide a visual foil to the graceful Eichlers.

■ Stairs that would have taken us down to 30th Street have been covered with gunite and converted into a culvert. Somebody doesn't like walkers.

□ There are footpaths on this hill.

□ We follow the uppermost path that parallels Beacon, a street of townhouses and detached dwellings. The views between houses are exceptional. This enchanting area of the city is well worth the walk.

□ Next to 190 Beacon is a beautiful stairway. It's the Harry Stairs, which we approach from the Glen Park area on Walk 24. We could connect with that walk and go on to Chenery via Laidley Street; however, since we want to walk toward the Walter Haas Park, we continue southeast on Beacon and turn right onto Digby.

□ Next to 54 Digby, a gate blocks us off from a paved culvert-shaped area descending to Beacon. If this paved section was once a continuation of the Harry Stairs up to Digby, then the Harry Stairs must have been the most magnificent San Francisco stairway of all.

□ We continue west on Digby to Addison. On the corner is the handsome John F. Shelley Fire Station 26, dedicated to the San Franciscan who was mayor from 1964 to 1968.

□ On our right is Walter Haas Park with a tot lot, basketball and handball courts, lots of benches, grass, birch trees, and a view. From here we get a unique look at the Sutro Tower and the curving lines of the Bay Bridge.

HARRY STREET

☐ We walk the park path behind the fire station and look down on Billy Goat Hill at Castro and 30th, purchased with city Open Space Funds in 1976. The steep grade prevents descent.

☐ The stairway around the children's slide areas takes us up to Diamond Heights Boulevard between Diamond Street and Addison.

☐ We continue along Diamond Heights Boulevard toward the shopping center to the north and take Gold Mine Drive to the right. Near the corner next to 70 Gold Mine a stairway/walkway leads us to the 28th and Douglass cul-de-sac, completing the circle of one of the most beautiful walks we've taken.

23

DIAMOND HEIGHTS TWO

Rocks, Minerals, and H₂O

Diamond Heights, 325 acres of craggy, hilly terrain, is impassable at several locations and difficult and expensive to build on, yet contains a variety of modest to luxurious homes, townhouses, apartments, and condominiums, many of which were built after World War II when federal redevelopment money became available for construction. Trees are everywhere but in the yards, volcanic rocks challenge the gardener. Here we can appreciate the problem that grading was, is, and forevermore will be, and why there are so many stairways here (even with some of them inexplicably blocked).

■ We begin at the corner of Diamond Heights Boulevard and Gold Mine Drive and go south on Gold Mine past the multicolored concrete wall of St. Aidan's Episcopal Church. This section of Diamond Heights was one of the last to be developed, and the houses here date from the 1960s.

☐ Passing Topaz, we continue up one of the highest hills in San Francisco—679 feet above sea level—past an unmarked stairway between Nos. 156 and 158 which we deduce is Opalo Lane, apparently leading to a shopping center. On Gold Mine, there are empty spaces between houses that cry out to be stairways for direct descent to Christopher Playground on Diamond Heights Boulevard far below us.

☐ We find the intersection at Jade Place a good lookout station for a panoramic view of the Bay Bridge, skyscrapers, and many sailboats. A bit farther south on Gold Mine we can see Twin Peaks, the Mt. Sutro television tower, Mt. Davidson, and San Bruno Mountain. Then look far down to Glen Canyon Park and the wide corridor of O'Shaughnessy Boulevard.

☐ In the 1800s, Glen Canyon Park was the place for carnivals, parades, picnics, dances, and other amusements. A special Sunday treat was a canary trainer from the Cliff House who often ascended in a gas-filled balloon, or walked a tightrope across the canyon. There was also a zoo that featured bears, monkeys, and elephants. Around 1907, the Crocker Estates Company put in private tennis and basketball courts to rent to organizations. Because of this, neighborhood children had to play on the street. Local residents lobbied the city to purchase the land, and in 1922 the Board of Supervisors made the first payment on the 104 acres in Glen Canyon Park.

■ Returning to Topaz and bearing left at No. 243, we descend the Onique Stairway back to Gold Mine, cross it to continue the stairway down to Berkeley Way. Our view shifts to Highway 280 below, and to the hills on the San Francisco/San Mateo boundary. The pyramid-building Egyptians would have liked the geometric patterns of the homes in the distance.

☐ At Berkeley Way, pause in the descent to note the extraordinary rock formation next to 80 Crags Court Way. We turn to Diamond Heights Boulevard and walk south on the righthand side parallel to Glen Canyon Park. On Arbor, we turn left, and again left onto Hiliritas Avenue, which was part of the original Diamond Heights redevelopment plan, accounting for the unusually large lots here. A few Queen Anne and Edwardian homes are scattered throughout this neighborhood.

☐ We continue on Hiliritas to Conrad, thus leaving Diamond Heights to enter the Glen Park neighborhood.

■ We turn right on Conrad, left on Arbor, right on Diamond Street, walking past Sussex. Next to 2611 Diamond, an obscure and pretty footpath, framed by a pepper tree, berries, and bougainvillea, takes us to 30 Surrey, a seven-room house built in 1902 by the present occupant's father. The black walnut tree in its yard continues to bear fruit, but the activities of past childhood—catching frogs in Glen Canyon stream, hunting rabbits in the hills, and even hiding out in a cave on Red Rock Hill for a week after running away from home at age thirteen—are no longer possible.

☐ If hunger strikes, we detour left on Surrey and right on Chenery for comestibles. Satisfied, walk west to Diamond, and follow its windy way to Diamond Heights—a no-nonsense twenty-minute walk back to the beginning. We can, if we choose, hook onto Walk 22 and enjoy the Harry Street Stairway.

A Twitton and A Bucket for Blackberries

After Mexico became independent of Spain in 1821, settlement and private ownership of California lands was encouraged by large grants awarded to high-ranking officials. In 1845, Rancho San Miguel, which included present-day Glen Park, was given to José Noe, the last *alcalde,* or mayor, under Mexican rule.

After the Mexican War, Noe became an official in the government of the United States in 1846. Although his land holdings were guaranteed, he lost them in various disputes and they were eventually sold to developers and homestead associations.

Three people who played important roles in the Glen Park community bought large sections of Rancho San Miguel: Francois Pioche, a Frenchman who later established the famous Poodle Dog Restaurant, a San Francisco landmark for more than a century; Adolph Sutro, from Bavaria, who left a legacy of planted areas and parks in the western part of the city (Mt. Sutro was part of the Rancho); and Behrend Joost, a German who in 1891 built the electric streetcars that connected Glen Park to the rest of San Francisco.

In the 1850s, Glen Park became a dairy area when the city condemned the dairies in Cow Hollow (Walk 8) after a cholera outbreak and ordered them moved to a less populated area.

The Crocker Estate Company eventually gained control of Glen Park and described it as "a veritable Switzerland." Their ads in a 1908 newspaper exhorted people wanting to make money to buy improved lots in Glen Park. These cost $300 to $500 each, and could be paid off at the rate of $5 per month.

Glen Canyon Park was bought by San Francisco in 1922, and the surrounding area was sold for homesites.

■ We begin our walk at the Glen Park Library at 653 Chenery Street, near Diamond. This one-room storefront was built especially for the Library by William Tietz, a lifelong member of the community, an avid library patron, and an architect. He tore down a Victorian house to make room for a new library building on the site. His wife Valborg showed equally strong feelings about libraries and took an active role in the project.

☐ We walk west to Diamond, turn right and follow it north to Sussex, noticing along the way a hodgepodge of architectural styles, including many Queen Anne rowhouses, intact as well as modified.

☐ We turn left onto Sussex toward Conrad and walk a few feet. Just before we come to the end of the block, we are at the "twitton," Poppy Lane. A "twitton" is what the English call an alley or a narrow right-of-way.

POPPY LANE

☐ We turn right and enjoy an instant contrast to city streets—in spring, a riot of colors and in fall, more sedate—a treasure of blackberries waiting for buckets.

☐ The lane is blocked off by an apartment house at Sussex, so we continue to Diamond.

☐ On Diamond, turn right, then left to Sussex to Bemis, and follow Bemis northeast to the Amatista Lane Stairway, which takes us up to Everson, the most strenuous section of the walk. A shopping center was proposed for the triangle near the top of the stairs, but residents opposed it, and the area is now a small park.

☐ We are now on Everson, one of the oldest sections of the Diamond Heights Redevelopment Area. We learn from a resident that her home and the house at 50 Everson, which was made with lumber from the 1939 World's Fair on Treasure Island, were the only two structures on the street twenty-five years ago.

☐ We make a right turn off Everson to bear north on Beacon.

☐ The Harry Stairway begins between 190 and 200 Beacon. It is surrounded by tall trees and almost hidden behind high vegetation where it begins. There is a country atmosphere about this stairway; the air is redolent with pine and Scotch broom.

☐ The long, wooden, and rather steep Harry Stairway is one of the most beautiful in the city. The homes alongside, with their decks and wide windows, set an individual style. African daisies, ivy, geraniums, fuchsia, wild onion, pittisporum, yucca, lily of the Nile, and pyracantha make a festival of color.

☐ From the top of the stairway, Yerba Buena Island to the east and the spires of St. Paul's Cathedral toward the north are clearly visible. As we descend, the Bay Bridge and downtown San Francisco emerge.

☐ The Harry Stairway ends at Laidley and we turn right. At the corner is a spacious Queen Anne home, a citadel surrounded by more modest structures. We continue on Laidley, turn left on Miguel, and right on Chenery for coffee.

☐ After an interval of conversation, return to the end of the Harry Stairway and continue north on Laidley. We make another left on 30th to Castro, and take the stairs at Castro and Day streets.

☐ Now, it's right on Day to Noe—right on Noe to 30th—left on 30th to Harper—and right onto Harper, ending at Laidley, where we turn left, then left again onto Miguel, and right on Chenery.

☐ We have ceased to worry when confronted with hills. Press on!

☐ As recently as the 1970s, the hills here were vacant and residents used them for picnics and kite-flying. Now only a portion of the hillside is kept as a green zone. By day, the streets are choked with cars parked by commuters using the Glen Park BART station.

☐ In spite of this, Glen Park is unique. Community spirit and neighborhood individuality are shown through an active weekly newspaper, *The Citizen*, by fervent support for the local library, and in the existence of many thriving small businesses nearby.

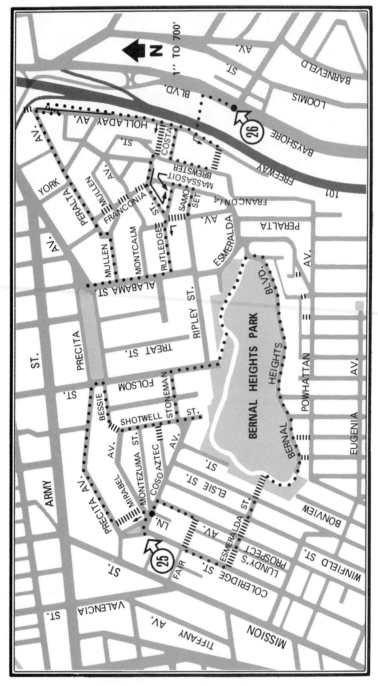

MAP L

25 □ Summer, Fall, and Late Spring
26 □ Dogs, Cats, Children, and the Remaining Eve

Summer, Fall,
and Late Spring

Bernal Heights neighborhood is bounded by four broad and busy thoroughfares—the Bayshore Freeway on the east, Mission Street on the west, Army Street on the north, and Alemany on the south. The rancho of almost 4000 acres granted by the Mexican government to José Bernal in 1839 passed from him to his attorneys, who divided the grant into building lots. In the 1860s and 1870s, the area was dairy land.

Many of the Bernal Heights street names have Civil War associations—Banks, Winslow, Putnam, Army, Moultrie, Sumter, Lincoln. . . . Eugenia, however, was named for the daughter of a tollkeeper on San Bruno Road.

I experimented with three different walks in this benign sun pocket, but still felt a kink in shoulder and knee. The walks didn't flow properly until I tried the following itinerary, which when traced on a map forms itself into a foot in a boot! It brings to mind Rainer Maria Wilke's poetic description of a walker: "his step was . . . unusually light, full of remembrance of earlier walking."

■ We begin on Coso Avenue near Coleridge. Several Queen Anne rowhouses on the east side are newly painted. The Victorian stick-style house at 130 Coso, which also bears the address of No. 1 Lundys Lane, has a corner rectangular bay window. Behind it, at No. 9 Lundys Lane, is a flat-front Italianate positioned strangely—its side faces the street.

☐ We walk across Coso to Mirabel and descend the narrow stairway next to 9 Mirabel to Precita. We turn right to see the siding of No. 189 abloom with painted images of the Beatles!

☐ We turn right off Precita at Folsom to Bessie, a cul-de-sac of gabled roofs and remodeled turn-of-the-century houses, most of which are Queen Anne and Edwardian. Most interesting are the "skinnies" at 14, 16, 20, and 24 Bessie Street. They are each on a parcel only 12½ feet wide—exactly *half* the usual house lot in the city.

■ The Shotwell Stairway begins between 15 and 5 Bessie. We go up the stairway to Mirabel, a cul-de-sac tagged onto Shotwell, and go south on Shotwell. Nos. 1400, 1429, 1435, and 1437 Shotwell were probably camp cottages built for earthquake refugees after 1906. In passing by the Aztec Stairway next to 1434 Shotwell, we notice 74 Aztec, a flat-front Italianate which might have been built as early as 1870. An informant at the Water Department tells me that the initial connection was made April 25, 1901, for John McLaughlin; the house may well have been moved there from some original site.

☐ No. 1502 Shotwell is set in a field of blackberries! Upon closer inspection, it appears to be a barn that has been attractively enlarged. One of its adornments is a striking artist's studio window.

☐ We continue to Stoneman, passing another house in a field that may contain barking dogs. Now we're at the foot of Bernal Hill, one of the city's 43, now occupied by eucalyptus and wild amaryllis, along with a microwave station belonging to Pacific Telephone. Shall we follow the footpath onto the hill? It can be muddy in spring and winter, and calls for hiking shoes in other seasons. Take the more secure route: Stoneman to Folsom, where we make a right turn and go southeast through the park to Bernal Heights Boulevard.

☐ We walk on the South Bernal Heights Boulevard footpath, 325 feet above sea level, enjoying the panoramic view of the city. In 1876, there was a rumor of gold quartz in the hill.

☐ The red Valerian and California poppies bloom late in this area. Continue south toward Carver. Walking the footpath on the south side allows a view of this "paper street," unpaved and ending abruptly. Candlestick Park and the KYA radio tower on Candlestick Hill are on our distant left. Close by on our left is a windmill in a backyard.

■ On the Boulevard across from 40 Prentiss is a stone retaining wall all by itself. Farther along is the thriving Bernal Heights Community Garden.

☐ No. 66 Anderson has characters from Lewis Carroll's *Alice in Wonderland* carved around the art-glass window. There are Alice, the Red Queen, the Mad Hatter, the White Rabbit, the Caterpillar sitting on a mushroom smoking a hookah, and the Mock Turtle. The carving is certainly a most personal signature of the owner of the house. If we should meet one day while I'm walking by, I'll dispense with "nice day" and talk about important things like Alice's view of geography. "London is the capital of Paris, and Paris the capital of Rome, and Rome. . ." says Alice. "Oh, my ears and whiskers, how late it's getting," replies the White Rabbit. Carved around another window is a female nude reclining among acanthus leaves.

☐ The renovated 1929 cottage at 168 Moultrie has a cedar-shingled exterior and a detailed rosette near the top. Surrounding the structure is a rock garden with desert plantings that screen the house from traffic.

☐ We continue past the Andover Stairway. Directly south from Bocana, we see circular Holly Park. We persist on Bernal Heights Boulevard to the Esmeralda Stairway. Red-hot poker and pampas grass grow nearby. A kestrel flies above us as we descend. He is looking for grasshoppers, while we are looking at a house painted French military blue with old rose trim.

■ Try the two slides in Esmeralda Park between Winfield and Elsie

SHOTWELL STREET

(they have been de-slitherized for the safety of the little ones).

☐ We continue downward to Prospect and walk a few feet to our left to a fenced lot. The lessee, a rose fancier and historian, has planted autumn damask roses, famous in ancient Rome and used extravagantly by Nero, wood hyacinths, Rembrandt tulips, and other almost forgotten varieties of historical blooms to be used as cut flowers that he sells to the flower market.

☐ We go back to the stairway and down to Lundys Lane. This small section has exposed cliffs that are full of fennel in spring, houses in many different conditions, and trees. The height of the structures, most from the 1880s and 1890s, bestows an ambience of continuity and charm. No. 17 is one of the oldest in northwest Bernal Heights and is on its original homestead goat farm. It has been stretched from a simple gabled thin clapboard to a roomy two-story eight-room structure. The front is No. 34 Prospect.

☐ We turn right at Coleridge, at the bottom of the stairs onto the Fair path to Prospect. We turn left on Prospect and walk to Coso. No. 23 Prospect, an architect-designed house, dominates the block; its arresting design features an outsized front window and weathered siding. Two blocks left on Coso is the beginning of our walk.

Dogs, Cats, Children, and the Remaining Eve of Adam's Rib

East Bernal Heights is above a vertical, crazed network of overpasses and underpasses for automobiles which telescopes the history of San Francisco transportation.

In the beginning were the Ohlone Indians, the earliest settlers of the Bay Area of whom we have records. During the sixteenth century, the Spanish and the English explored the ocean and the Bay in ships. In the eighteenth century, the padres came north from Mexico, establishing missions along the way of what came to be El Camino Real. Now Highway 82 faithfully follows most of this historic path, including the upland winter route around Alameda de las Pulgas in San Mateo County that avoided the wet and muddy flatlands.

The Gold Rush of 1849 strained all modes of transportation into the city. Ferry boats transported men and goods between San Francisco and the North and East Bays. Horses and carriages, later trains, carried passengers from San Francisco south down the Peninsula. The city's first streetcar line was built in 1857, and in 1873 Andrew Hallidie tried out the cable car that would make areas like Nob Hill easily accessible.

In 1926, the U. S. Post Office awarded contracts for delivery of air mail to private individuals, and the city began a search for an airport site. In 1927, Mills Field was dedicated as San Francisco's municipal airport. Some people still remember Mills Field as a favorite spot for watching pilots take off in their two-seaters to perform daredevil stunts. In 1930, the city bought *all* of the Mills estate, over a million acres, for development as an air terminal.

As tourism increased, the stable population also grew. Bayshore Highway was dedicated in 1929. Heavy industry began moving into South San Francisco, World War II accelerated the movement of men and machines, Superhighway 101 was built in the late 1940s, and Highway 280 in the 1950s.

In the meantime, Alemany, Mission, and Army crisscrossed and the area became a tangle of interlocking auto and truck highways, each more super than the last, discouraging timid pedestrians from trying to find a way amid the twentieth-century maze.

Above all is Bernal Heights, part of the Rancho de las Salinas y Potrero Nuevo, granted to José Cornelio de Bernal in 1830 by the Mexican government.

In the 1860s, the rancho—one league square, approximately 4000 acres—was subdivided, and Vitus Wackenreuder made a survey of Bernal Heights. Wackenreuder plotted his streets narrow and his lots small—23 by 76 feet. Most of them do not meet city specifications of minimum size. To this day, the city does not maintain the "streets" or stairs in Bernal Heights. The east slope exceeds forty-five percent grade in many places, and its geological composition has hazardous landslide potential—another reason for the city not to accept responsibility for the streets. Also, special soil studies would be needed before they could be paved—at enormous expense, considering the relatively small number of people living here today. Hence we find railroad-tie steps partially sunk into the ground, unpaved areas slippery and muddy during the winter rains, and everything rather higgledy-piggledy.

After subdivision, the first group of settlers, predominantly Irish, farmed the land. Dairy ranching was the first extensive industry in Bernal Heights. Wakes were the most popular social gatherings, along with the telling of stories by "them as had the gift." One of the more famous events of the time was when the Widow O'Brien's best milch cow was taken to the city pound. All the neighbors came to her defense to get it back.

German and Italian settlers followed the Irish. During World War II, people from all over the United States came to work in the nearby naval shipyards.

■ We begin our walk on the west side of Bayshore Boulevard at Oakdale and walk north to the end of the block. We turn left and ascend Faith pedestrian overpass, a testimonial to grassroots action by Bernal Heights residents who fought for access across the freeway.

□ As we climb up to Holladay, we see lots of shrubbery, grasses, and weeds of variegated shapes and volumes. Pythagoras, I defy you to theorize these forms!

□ Along the way, the noise level of traffic rises and falls. According to a Bernal Heights East Slope study in 1979, noise levels here generally exceed the 55 decibels permissible in San Francisco.

■ On Holladay, we turn left and walk to Joy Street, to a wooden platform that says No. 14 where we ascend a few wooden steps. It's easy to imagine Biblical prophets and sheep here, approving the hilly field of grasses and an S-shaped border of color—varieties of geraniums, lupins, poppies, and two healthy pines. Although Joy is a public street, the stairway, path, and plantings were established by the owner of No. 14.

□ We continue alongside 16, 18, and 20 Joy, all originally flat-front Italianates from the 1870s and 1880s. The fragrance of the salvia near No. 18 intensifies the feeling that we are walking on private grounds. Everything feels rural—a hidden urban treat.

□ We follow along discontinuous railroad-tie steps past No. 20 to Brewster—just below the community gardens—and turn right. There are no square corners here and the signpost seems to lean, so we ask a resident to point out Costa, where we turn right and come back to Holladay, then left for one "block" to Rutledge, next to the fire hydrant.

□ The Rutledge Stairway that we will walk up was built by Andy Husari, who lived at No. 19 until 1983. The rains of 1981 washed out the previous stairs, so he patiently hand-wrought the present ones and continued them up Franconia to Mullen.

☐ No. 19 was built in 1906 as one of the earthquake refugee cottages that abound in the area. Because the soils become so saturated during the rainy seasons, most of the houses originally had a pump or wind-mill to raise the water. Mr. Husari remembers mushrooms growing in his basement when he moved in. Because the area has the best weather conditions in the city, he had a harvest of twenty ears of corn one Christmas. He planted the adjoining lot, to our right, with native shrubs and trees—coffeeberry, toyon, redwood, spruce, as well as mountain fire and Torrey pine.

■ We go off Holladay up the Rutledge Stairway (which is public but looks private).

☐ We walk to the landing next to 200 Rutledge for a grand view of the north. From east to west we see San Francisco General Hospital, the Tischman Building at 525 Market Street, the darkly-colored Shaklee Building, Coit Tower, and former St. Joseph's Hospital near Corona Heights. 210 Rutledge has almost this same extraordinary view through the window.

☐ Arriving at Massasoit, we double around, left to Franconia and view the industrial scene of San Francisco and the East Bay.

☐ We turn right on Franconia to Samoset, and right again. Here at the "corner" is the Peralta Stairway, and the super-grand view of all. Today the light is perfect. We see Twin Peaks and the Mt. Sutro television tower to the west, Golden Gate Bridge and Mt. Tamalpais to the north, Angel Island and Coit Tower farther east, and. . . toward the southeast, one of the four Pacific Gas & Electric Company natural gas holders that contain from 10 to 17 million cubic feet of gas.

☐ We descend to Rutledge, which has an especially interesting assort-ment of flat-front structures in differing states of repair, and a large trailer with a roof sculpture. It moves, it stretches. Aha! It's a live goat!

☐ We turn left on Rutledge toward Alabama Street's goodly share of Victorian rowhouses. We turn right on Alabama and walk to Precita Park, which has a pleasant array of children's swings, revolving dishes, benches, and tables.

■ We stop here for a few minutes to imagine alighting from a coach. This park was once a stagecoach stop in the days following the Gold Rush. Immediately after the Earthquake, Precita Park was a refugee camp.

☐ Across the street is Le Conte School, which has the most beautiful mural wall in the city. Called "The Spirit of Mankind," it combines ex-travagant colors in abstract shapes and naturalistic forms.

☐ We go back on Alabama to Mullen and turn left. 15 Mullen is Bernal Heights' answer to Watts Towers, the famous Los Angeles landmark fabricated from scraps of metal, cement, and glass over a period of many years by Simon Rodia. In front of the small residence are three trunks encased in cement, inlaid with mosaic, granite, polished marble, tile, shells, and glass balls. The embellishments are all "found" objects, and, like the Watts Towers, the project takes as long as it will take.

☐ We turn left on Peralta, which curves right, and walk for two blocks to York. No. 1619 York is a layered blue house with staggered windows.

☐ Continue on upper Peralta. This neighborhood teems with dogs, cats, and children. It has the feeling of a homemade muslin dress, perfect for chores and get togethers, but not suitable for the city.

☐ A stunning group of Queen Anne rowhouses is at Peralta and Hampshire Streets. It could be 1880—until we round the curve at Peralta and Holladay and collide with 1984.

■ The Peralta Stairway goes down to the freeway and around the back of the industrial sites. But continue toward the right on the upper level of Holladay. The elaborate Queen Annes are here on Wright Street.

☐ We descend small Eve Stairway, the remains of the original couple—Adam disappeared when the freeway was built—to the lower level of Holladay. Adam, Eve, Joy, Faith—an atmosphere is set.

☐ There is a blue "dollhouse" at 290 Holladay, and one expects little people to come forth through the door.

☐ We continue on Holladay to Faith, ready to descend in one fell swoop to the twentieth century.

☐ We cross Bayshore Boulevard at the Faith overpass. Look up and marvel at Bernal Heights East, battered but not completely sabotaged by the effects of the freeway. Unimproved streets have been further disconnected, homes abandoned, Peralta Ridge leveled and used as freeway fill, access to jobs and shopping made difficult. Bernal Heights East—so close to the artifacts of commerce, yet so far from it in spirit.

List of Stairways

"So all right," he cried, and we agreed.

Making the stairway list has been the most difficult task of all. There is always another stairway lurking ahead. But in every fairy tale, the completion of a very difficult task deserves a reward (perhaps a beautiful walking day).

Since this is an informal book, the ratings I have given the stairways are based purely on what struck me most during a walk—steepness, length, location, altitude, or beauty—and any combination in between.

No single factor can sum up the character of a stairway. It may be a hundred steps (Diamond and 22nd Street) but easy, or thirty steps and difficult (Collingwood Street). There are charming stairways (Pemberton) or utilitarian stairways (Stonestown). We have elegant stairways (Alta Plaza Park) and we have rustic ones (Joy). We have stairways bordered by trees, shrubs, flowers, stones, broken glass, railings, Victorian houses, and lean-tos.

Stairways are difficult to push into categories—it seems easier to classify neighborhoods than stairways. Forest Hill and Forest Knolls are unusual in settings and stairways. Golden Gate Heights and Noe Valley have well designed networks of stairways and retaining walls. Diamond Heights has series of very long stairways. Telegraph Hill and Russian Hill have little alleys and many houses that have no access to a street. Living along Filbert or Greenwich stairways is an incentive to purchase lightweight furniture and futons. Russian Hill, surrounded by other hill neighborhoods, gives a feeling of greater separation with its cul-de-sacs within cul-de-sacs (Vallejo and Florence). Upper Market is an unusual conglomerate of leveled, fenced-off, or permanently closed-off stairways. Mono, Hattie, Copper are being nibbled and shrunk by builders so that the area is a laboratory in gauging the growth of the city. Bernal Heights is a raggle-taggle assortment of streets that energetically fan out in several directions. (The patterns will stimulate any dancer's imagination.) Pacific Heights is a wonderful contrast. The plan is controlled, the outlines orderly, the stairways purposefully designed.

The range of views in each neighborhood is exhilarating and subtle; the ambience indicative of what the neighborhood has to offer.

Above all, this is a participatory book. The fun is in the walking, in the conversations struck up along the way, and in the marvelous views of an extraordinary city. Make personal notes beside each listing and send in new discoveries as you find them.

■ **Ratings.** Here is the rating system—strictly my own—that I used in rating the 330-odd stairways listed here. If you disagree with any of my ratings, or find any invisible or unknown stairways, please send a postcard, care of the publisher.

5 □ The Scheherazade category. These stairways surprise the walker, initially and forever after. They may be elegant or rustic, they may be short or long. But they exhibit variety, stir the imagination, and delight

the senses. One can only love them madly, these Scheherazades.

4 ☐ Impressive qualities with minor shortcomings and one outstanding aspect, or an extremely attractive section.

3 ☐ Little known but deserves wider recognition because of the environs, man-made or natural. Neighborhood generally very attractive.

2 ☐ Intrinsic to neighborhood history and ambience. Well-trodden. In most cases, the architectural context rates considerably higher than the stairway itself, or the view may be worth the visit. It's a pretty straightforward stairway of no great beauty.

1 ☐ A No. 1 stairway may be so boring that you'll fall asleep on the first landing.

* An * stair might well be worth visiting if it were located elsewhere—for example, in a safe neighborhood. This stairway is only for the knowledgeable resident, the wary aficionado.

■ **Anza Vista.** A neighborhood surrounding the University of San Francisco complex. Small well-kept homes from the fifties and the Victorian era are part of this area.

2 ☐ Arguello/Anza & Edward into Rossi Recreation Center. *Large granite planter bowls at entrance of two granite stairways.*

2 ☐ Dicha Alley/Lupine & Wood. *Useful and used.*

2 ☐ Ewing/at Nos. 196–200, to Anza near Collins. *Ewing Court was a baseball field at one time. Clever.*

4 ☐ Lone Mountain/from 401 Parker to Beaumont & Stanyan. *Long twitton, trees, church spires, views of Angel Island and west; nice series of Victorians on McAllister off Parker.*

■ **Bayview.** Some historic buildings in this neighborhood.

* Bayview Park. *All concrete.*
* Gilroy Street/Jamestown.
* LaSalle/Mendall & Lane.
* Quesada/Newhall & 3rd Street.
* Thornton/3rd Street & Latona.

■ **Bernal Heights.** A neighborhood of blue collar workers, lawyers, and artists.

4 ☐ Andover/Powhattan & Bernal Heights Blvd. *Defies description. Homespun array and diversity. View.*

2 ☐ Aztec/Shotwell & Stoneman. *Stoneman was a Union general in the Civil War.*

3 ☐ Brewster Stairway & Footpath/Rutledge, Costa & Mullen. *It's a kick, individualistic: the railing is a tree branch.*

2 ☐ Cortland/Prospect & Santa Marina. *Says, "Please walk on me."*

2 ☐ Coso Avenue/Prospect & Winfield. *View; cars from private driveway have to cross the stairs.*

3 ☐ Ellsworth and Bernal Heights Peak. *Left-over stone stairway. Refreshing view..*

4 ☐ Esmeralda/Winfield to Prospect to Lundys Lane to Coleridge.

4 ☐ Eugenia/Prospect & Winfield. *Among trees.*

1 ☐ Eve Stairway/upper & lower Holladay/Wright & Peralta. *A wraith of itself.*

3 ☐ Fair Avenue/Coleridge & Lundys Lane. *Rebuilt in more noble proportions. View.*

2 ☐ Faith Stairway/Bayshore & Holladay. *Part of a pedestrian overpass; an opportunity to hear increases in decibels from auto traffic.*

3 ☐ Faith/Brewster & Holladay. *Defies categorization.*

3 ☐ Franconia/Mullen & Montcalm. *Wooden, short. Shrubbery and trees alongside. View.*

3 ☐ Franconia/Rutledge. *Built by Robert McManus, 1974. Walkers use it to continue on footpath to the right.*

1 ☐ Holladay/Peralta & Adam.

4 ☐ Holladay/Peralta & Bayshore. *View. The link between an isolated, urban neighborhood and the main traffic arteries north and south.*

2 ☐ Holly Park/Bocana.

2 ☐ Holly Park/Highland.

2 ☐ Holly Park/Murray.

2 ☐ Holly Park/Park. *Across from muraled Junipero Serra School.*

5 ☐ Joy/Holladay & Brewster. *Rural. Special. Testament to grassroots participation. Stairway, path, plantings established by Bea Hendon.*

3 ☐ Kingston/Coleridge & Prospect. *Semblance of floating stairs. Railing. Rock formation on side plus a long footpath.*

3 ☐ Mayflower/Franconia. *Perhaps. Next to 500 Franconia. Belongs to the city. One of those marvelous anomalies that go nowhere.*

3 ☐ Mirabel/at No. 11, to Precita. *Hidden. Extremely narrow.*

3 ☐ Moultrie/Bernal Heights Blvd. & Powhattan. *Truly hidden and rural. First decisive victory of the Revolution was at Ft. Moultrie, S.C., in 1776.*

3 □ Mullen/Franconia. *Mullen is a fanciful land-locked 'street' in some spots.*

3 □ Peralta/Rutledge & Montcalm. *The kind of urban stairway that makes one chuckle and grin and happy to have discovered it; continues to Mullen as path.*

4 □ Peralta/Rutledge & Samoset. *Extraordinary view.*

1 □ Richland/Mission & San Jose.

3 □ Rosenkranz/Chapman & Powhattan. *Wooden stairs.*

4 □ Rutledge/Holladay & Mullen. *Handhewn by Andy Husari. Built, then rebuilt after '81–'82 rain damage. Adjacent native trees, shrubs planted by Husari.*

3 □ Shotwell/Mirabel & Bessie. *Hidden; you wouldn't think to look for it. 1906 earthquake cottages on Shotwell. 12.5-foot-wide lots on Bessie.*

3 □ Tompkins/Putnam & Nevada. *Stairway in much better condition than nearby fence. New tree plantings. View of the industrial side of the city.*

3 □ Virginia/Eugenia & Winfield. *Part of a stairway series from retaining wall to lower level.*

■ **Buena Vista.** An old conservative neighborhood with large mansions and converted flats.

3 □ Alpine/Waller & Duboce. *Sidewalk stairway.*

3 □ Ashbury Terrace/at No. 64, near Piedmont. *Baker & Haight into Buena Vista Park.*

* Buena Vista East/Haight, into Buena Vista Park. *The stair would rate 4 in a more benign location.*

2 □ Buena Vista East/No. 437, into Buena Vista Park. *Wooden. One of a series of three.*

4 □ Buena Vista Terrace/Buena Vista East & Duboce into Buena Vista Park. *Ornament above entrance wall gives unusual effect. Curving steps. View.*

* Buena Vista West/Haight, into Buena Vista Park. *Lovely. One of thee early, beautiful San Francisco neighborhoods—but be careful in your wanderings.*

4 □ Buena Vista West & Java/into Buena Vista Park. *Wooden.*

* Central & Buena Vista West/into Buena Vista Park. *Stone stairway.*

3 □ DeForest/Beaver & Flint. *A stairway street, three feet wide and*

125 feet long, built around 1975. At the top is Corona Heights Park and a lot of exploring.

3 ☐ Duboce/Castro & Alpine. *Special. Twenty-five percent grade.*

3 ☐ Frederick & Buena Vista West/into Buena Vista Park. *Concrete, wide. Should be extended.*

4 ☐ Welland Lathrop Memorial Walk/into Buena Vista Park. *Across from 547 Buena Vista West. Pine trees, view. Lathrop was one of the early modern dancers & teachers in San Francisco.*

2 ☐ Lyon & Haight/into Buena Vista Park.

2 ☐ Park Hill & Buena Vista East/into Buena Vista Park.

4 ☐ Waller/Broderick & Buena Vista West. *Sidewalk stairway, easy risers. View of Mt. Diablo.*

* Waller/Broderick, into Buena Vista Park. *Garrett Eckbo was the architect of Buena Vista Park erosion control measures which include stairways. Work in progress. Hidden. View.*

■ **Chinatown.** A special combination of sounds, smells, and colors.

2 ☐ California/opposite No. 660, into St. Mary's Square. *A relatively low-rated stairway in a fascinating locale.*

3 ☐ Clay/Kearny & Grant, into Portsmouth Square.

■ **Diamond Heights.** A neighborhood of views, hills, and canyons.

4 ☐ Coralino/289 Amber to 92 Cameo. *Woodsy. White crown sparrows love it.*

* Diamond Heights Blvd./687 28th St.

3 ☐ Moffitt at Diamond. *A very necessary stairway corner.*

5 ☐ Onique/101 Berkeley—289 Berkeley—400 Gold Mine-Topaz. *Forty-five-degree view of San Francisco. Surroundings of eucalyptus, pine, canyons, hummingbirds. A four-tiered Chinese hopscotch walk.*

2 ☐ Opalo/160 Gold Mine to Christopher Park. *Christopher Park is next to Diamond Heights shopping center.*

2 ☐ Twenty-seventh Street/at No. 881 to 5150 Diamond Heights Blvd. *Adjoining Douglass Playground. Part of a long stairway outlined by trees. Nice access.*

■ **Dolores Heights.** A lovely, hilly neighborhood in the Mission.

5 ☐ Cumberland/Noe & Sanchez. *Very impressive.*

4 ☐ Cumberland/Sanchez & Church. *View. Hidden. Additional curving ramp and wall. Dense vegetation.*

5 ☐ Liberty/Noe & Rayburn. *Beautifully designed foliage plantings. Art Deco houses alongside. View to east and west.*

3 ☐ Nineteenth Street/over MUNI Metro into Dolores Park.

4 ☐ Sanchez/19th Street & Cumberland. *City-designed entrance stairway plus sidewalk stairs. Four large, fifty-year-old cedars alongside. View.*

5 ☐ Sanchez/Liberty & 21st Street. *Network of stairs, one of the most beautiful series in the city. View.*

4 ☐ Sanchez/Liberty & 21st Street.

5 ☐ Twentieth Street/Noe. *Impressive. Backdrop of high curving wall.*

5 ☐ Twentieth Street/Sanchez. *Two stairways descending gracefully. Views. Enters a cul-de-sac that connects with Noe stairway and ramp.*

■ **Downtown.** A neighborhood of significance and diversity.

2 ☐ Ellis/Market, down to BART/MUNI Metro station. *Rather steep.*

1 ☐ Embarcadero/Market, down into BART/MUNI Metro station. *Built in 1973. Concrete stairway and wall, brushed aluminum railings. Interesting new edifices of financial district.*

2 ☐ Market/down into BART/MUNI Metro station. *Very steep.*

3 ☐ Montgomery/Market, down to BART/MUNI Metro station. *In the financial district among historic and nonhistoric highrises. Bubbled tile wall.*

1 ☐ Powell/Geary, into Union Square. *Magicians, music, skits, street artists: lots of local color.*

4 ☐ Powell/Market, down to BART/MUNI Metro station. *Wide esplanade into Swig Pavilion and visitors information center, a slice of Hogarth scenes and people.*

1 ☐ Stockton/Geary, into Union Square.

1 ☐ Stockton/Post, into Union Square.

2 ☐ Stockton/Sutter & Bush. *Over the Stockton Tunnel.*

2 ☐ Van Ness/Market, down to MUNI Metro station.

■ **Edgehill.** The steepness of the hill limits the number of homes on this street that winds up to the summit.

3 ☐ Edgehill/Kensington—Granville—Allston—Dorchester.

5 ☐ Pacheco/Merced & Vasquez. *Echoes the Grand Stairway to the north.*

3 ☐ Vasquez/opposite 233 Kensington—Merced.

3 ☐ Verdun/Claremont—Lennox.

■ **Eureka Valley.** This neighborhood has a community organization active since 1881, a large gay population, fine Victorians, and the Castro—a movie palace from 1923.

3 ☐ Caselli/Clayton & Market.

2 ☐ Church Street Footbridge/19th Street over MUNI tracks.

3 ☐ Collingwood/20th & 21st Streets. *It helps not to look up.*

1 ☐ Douglass/19th. *If someone insists on a stair, you can't stop them.*

4 ☐ Douglass/20th Street & Corwin. *Delightful discovery. Trees alongside.*

3 ☐ Douglass/Corwin. *Solution to elevating and lowering streets.*

2 ☐ Prosper/16th Street & Pond. *Behind Eureka branch library—an inviting place, a fine book collection.*

2 ☐ Romain/Douglass. *Upper to lower levels.*

2 ☐ Seward/Douglass & 19th Street. *Three sets of stairs. Enriches street by adding another level of viewing. Also very useful.*

3 ☐ Twenty-first Street/Castro & Collingwood.

4 ☐ Twenty-second Street/Collingwood & Diamond.

3 ☐ Twenty-second Street/Collingwood & Castro. *Profuse plantings.*

■ **Excelsior.** A stable neighborhood of diverse ethnic groups, and stairways reminiscent of the everyday kind in European towns.

2 ☐ Athens/Avalon & Valmar.

2 ☐ Campus Lane/Princeton & Burrows.

3 ☐ Dwight/Goettingen & Hamilton. *View. Very long.*

* Excelsior/at No. 1021 into McLaren Park.

3 ☐ Goettingen and Dwight.

2 ☐ Kenney Alley/at 646 London to Mission. *Difficult to find.*

4 ☐ Munich/Ina & Excelsior. *Hidden. View. One of the newer (1977) stairways in the city.*

1 ☐ Naglee/Alemany & Cayuga.

4 ☐ Peru/Athens & Valmar. *Aggregate and railroad ties, designed by R. Schadt. Great views.*

1 ☐ Restani/Cayuga & Alemany. *Practical. Hidden—only the residents know it.*

* Trumbull/Mission & Craut.

■ **Forest Hill.** The City has recently accepted responsibility for maintaining the non-regulation streets and sidewalks of this neighborhood.

4 ☐ Castenada/at No. 140 to 334 Pacheco to 5 Sotelo. *Adjacent is a Maybeck house with delightful details: carved grapevines along the eaves.*

5 ☐ Montalvo/376 Castenada—San Marcos—9th Ave.—Mendosa. *Variety in terrain, architecture, and "custom-made" stairways.*

5 ☐ Pacheco/Magellan & 249 Castenada. *Grandest and most elegant of all San Francisco stairways.*

4 ☐ Alton/Pacheco at No. 400 to 60 Ventura.

5 ☐ Alton/8th Ave. & 20 Ventura.

2 ☐ San Marcos/Dorantes. *Rounding a corner.*

5 ☐ Santa Rita/at No. 60, to upper Pacheco at No. 349. *View of Marin.*

2 ☐ Twelfth Avenue/Magellan & Dorantes.

■ **Forest Knolls.**   A neighborhood heavily forested with eucalyptus.

4 ☐ Ashwood Stairway/Clarendon, 95 & 101 Warren. *View across to Mt. Davidson. Among the trees.*

4 ☐ Blairwood Lane/109 Warren, 95 & 101 Crestmont. *View. Green railings which camouflages it among pine and acacia floating stairs. Over-realistic view of TV tower.*

3 ☐ Glenhaven Lane/Oak Park & 191 Christopher.

5 ☐ Oakhurst Lane/Warren & Crestmont. *View of ocean. Difficult. Longest continuous stairway to highest elevation in San Francisco. Eucalyptus forest.*

■ **Glen Park.**   Cows roamed the meadowland in this neighborhood in the 1880s.

3 ☐ Amatista Lane/Bemis & Everson. *Hardy.*

2 ☐ Arlington/at No. 439 to San Jose. *Hidden.*

2 ☐ Burnside/Bosworth.

2 ☐ Chilton/Bosworth & Lippard.

2 ☐ Cuvier/San Jose & Bosworth.

3 ☐ Diamond/Bosworth & Monterey into BART station. *View. Variety of textures in walks and stairs.*

2 ☐ Diamond/Moffitt.

2 ☐ Hamerton/Bosworth & Mangels.

1 ☐ Roanoke/San Jose & Arlington. *A walker's solution to freeway divisiveness.*

1 ☐ San Jose/Randall & Bosworth.

1 ☐ St. Mary's/San Jose & Arlington.

■ **Golden Gate Heights.** Carl Larsen from Denmark deeded this acreage to the city in 1928.

3 ☐ Aerial Way/475 Ortega & 801 Pacheco. *Much length. Ice plant to stabilize soil. Part of a network of stairways, all rated 4 or 5.*

2 ☐ Aloha and Lomita. *Part of a network, all highly rated.*

5 ☐ Cascade Walk/Ortega, Pacheco & Funston. *Secluded. Special.*

3 ☐ Crestwell/off Ortega.

3 ☐ Encinal Walk/14th & 15th Avenues.

3 ☐ Fanning Way/15th Avenue & Quintara. *Becomes part of a retaining wall that slopes.*

3 ☐ Fanning at 14th. *Curved corner with a view and high retaining wall on other side.*

4 ☐ Fifteenth Avenue/Kirkham & Lomita. *View.*

4 ☐ Fifteenth Avenue/Kirkham & Lawton. *Pine trees alongside. Walk up slowly.*

4 ☐ Fourteenth Avenue/Pacheco. *Very long trek up.*

4 ☐ Lomita/Kirkham & Lawton. *View of houses on stilts.*

4 ☐ Mandalay Lane/2001 14th & 15th Avenues & Pacheco. *Ocean view.*

5 ☐ Moraga/west from 12th, east from 17th Avenue. *Part of a network. High wall gives a feeling of timelessness. Cypress and pine alongside.*

4 ☐ Mount Lane/1795 14th Avenue & 1798 15th Avenue.

4 ☐ Noriega/15th Avenue & Sheldon Terrace. *Huge rock outcropping.*

4 ☐ Oriole Way/Pacheco & Cragmont. *Lots of foliage and long landings. View of houses on stilts.*

4 ☐ Ortega Way/14th & 1894 15th Avenue. *Very long and very practical. Ocean view. Ice plants on sides.*

4 ☐ Pacheco/15th Avenue. *View.*

2 ☐ Pacheco & 14th Avenue. *A snippet for rounding a corner.*

4 ☐ 500 Quintara/14th & 15th Avenues. *Great sunset viewing area. Double stairway a third of the way. Built 1928. View.*

3 ☐ Quintara at corner of 16th Avenue. *Nice curving wide rounded corner.*

5 ☐ Selma Way/477 Noriega & 564 Ortega. *View. High, high, high.*

3 ☐ Sixteenth Avenue/Kirkham & Lawton. *Stairway built before the surrounding houses.*

3 ☐ Sixteenth Avenue/Pacheco & Quintara. *Series of small stairways. Graceful.*

5 ☐ Twelfth Avenue/Cragmont, into Golden Gate Heights Park. *Cobblestone stairs.*

■ **Golden Gate Park.** Stairs still being built here.

3 ☐ Anglers Lodge/off Kennedy Drive, opposite Buffalo Paddock. Stone stairway.

3 ☐ Arboretum near Sunset Garden.

3 ☐ Children's Playground to Kezar Drive.

3 ☐ Conservatory (east of). *Dahlia gardens. Concrete stair.*

3 ☐ Fulton & 10th Avenue. *Wide railroad tie/blacktop stairs. Into play and rest area.*

3 ☐ Fulton & Arguello. *Curving railroad tie stairs and sides.*

3 ☐ Horseshoe Court. *Built in the thirties.*

3 ☐ Huntington Falls/top of Strawberry Hill to Stow Lake. *Railroad tie-and-chicken wire boxes filled with boulders and stones. A stairway for giants and a giant waterfall.*

2 ☐ Japanese Tea Garden to north side of Stow Lake.

2 ☐ South Drive near Murphy Windmill at Great Highway. *Continues to footpath.*

2 ☐ South Drive to Big Rec area.

2 ☐ South Drive to Stow Lake.

3 ☐ South Drive/intersection at Kennedy Drive. *Wooden. Leads to footpath.*

3 ☐ Stow Lake/south side, to south side Strawberry Hill. *Wooden stairs.*

5 ☐ Strawberry Hill/from top to Stow Lakeshore. *Fine view. Built of railroad ties, will connect with two new stairways, one on each side of Huntington Falls.*

■ **Land's End.** Great area for ocean breezes and beach.

4 ☐ Eagle's Point/Coastal Trail & the Ocean.

3 ☐ Land's End Stairway/lower footpath & Fort Miley parking.

4 ☐ Mile Rock/Coastal Trail & the Ocean. *One of the new stairways.*

5 ☐ Milestone Stairway/Merrie Way & Sutro Baths. *Sand ladder.*

4 ☐ Naval Memorial Stairway/48th Avenue & El Camino del Mar.

■ **Marina.** Development of this neighborhood was given impetus from the 1915 International Exposition.

3 ☐ Fort Mason/Bateria San Jose & Tier 4.

3 ☐ Fort Mason/Great Meadow to piers, opposite Bldg. E.

3 ☐ Fort Mason/Picnic Area & Tier 3.

4 ☐ Fort Mason/upper fort to Aquatic Park. *View.*

4 ☐ Jefferson/Beach, Hyde & Larkin.

■ **Mission.** One of the largest generic districts in San Francisco. Divided into more than a dozen sub-neighborhoods.

3 ☐ Seventeenth Street/Potrero & Bryant, into Franklin Square.

3 ☐ Sixteenth Street/Bryant, into Franklin Square.

2 ☐ Twenty-fourth Street/Mission, down into BART station.

■ **Mount Davidson.** A neighborhood encircling the highest point in San Francisco.

2 ☐ Balboa Park BART station.

2 ☐ Balboa Park/San Jose Avenue.

3 ☐ Bengal/Miraloma & Lansdale. *Wooden risers, concrete and cobblestone steps.*

3 ☐ Burlwood/Los Palmos. *Curving a corner.*

4 ☐ Dalewood Way, from Mt. Davidson. *Stone and moss stairways through nature trails of pine and eucalyptus.*

4 ☐ Detroit/Joost, Monterey & Hearst. *Very handy. A street stairway, crossing a main thoroughfare. Compare with Harry Street.*

3 ☐ Dorcas/222 Bella Vista & Myra.

2 ☐ Globe Alley/96 Cresta Vista to Hazelwood near Los Palmos. *Combination easement and stairway.*

2 ☐ Lulu Alley/Los Palmos & 450–500 Melrose. *Combination easement and stairway.*

4 ☐ Melrose/Teresita to Mangels to Sunnyside Playground. *Starts down from 195 Melrose. Lots of variety in the stair series. Melrose is a double street! The 800 block Teresita is across from 195 Melrose.*

3 ☐ Miraloma/Portola. *Goes to pedestrian skyway to West Portal neighborhood.*

3 ☐ Myra/95 Coventry & Dalewood. *Hidden. Curved and grooved lane.*

4 ☐ Rex/Juanita & Marne. *Fog, moss, stone, and fresh air.*

■ **Nob Hill.** A famous neighborhood well-known to tourists.

4 ☐ Joice/Pine, Sacramento, Powell & Stockton. *Graceful curve at Pine.*

2 ☐ Mason/southeast corner of California.

2 ☐ Priest/opposite 1350 Washington, to Clay. *Connects to Reid Stairway.*

2 ☐ Reid/Washington & Clay. *Connects to Priest Stairway.*

3 ☐ Taylor/California & Sacramento into Huntington Park.

4 ☐ Taylor/Pine & California. *Sidewalk stairway on both sides of the street, 235 steps.*

■ **Noe Valley.** An authentic neighborhood.

4 ☐ Castro/28th & Duncan. *Panoramic views. Franciscan rock formation. Wildlife haven. Strenuous walking.*

3 ☐ Castro/Day & 590 30th Streets. *We have non-streets and double streets intersecting; now it's stairways meeting. Adjacent Franciscan rock cliffs. Entrance to Glen Park neighborhood.*

5 ☐ Cumberland/Noe. *Cobblestone wall. Zigzag contour of stairs. View.*

3 ☐ 493 Day up to 2350 Castro. *Go up.*

3 ☐ Diamond/Valley. *Wildlife haven. Great moon-viewing lookout. Panoramic view.*

2 ☐ Duncan/Noe toward Sanchez. *Duncan is so steep that it is cut off from traffic at this point and further toward Diamond.*

3 ☐ Elizabeth/Hoffman & Grand View.

5 ☐ Harry/at 190 Beacon to Laidley. *Unusual wooden stairway that connects Noe Valley, Glen Park—maybe Diamond Heights, too. Very hidden. Built in 1932 by Eaton & Smith, contractors.*

4 ☐ Liberty/Sanchez & Church. *Stairways here. Very inviting area, lots of foliage.*

2 ☐ Sanchez/Cumberland.

4 ☐ Twenty-second Street/Church & Vicksburg. *Sidewalk stairway. If you feel you're sliding backward, it's because the steps slope backward. One of the steepest climbs in the city.*

3 ☐ Twenty-seventh Street/Castro & Newburg. *Views. Stairway at end of cul-de-sac blocked off.*

2 ☐ Valley/Castro to Noe. *Steep driveways show height of original street.*

■ **North Beach.** A neighborhood in transition from predominantly Italian settlers to Chinese.

2 ☐ Brenham Place/Washington & Kearny.

2 ☐ Romolo/Vallejo & Fresno, west of Kearny.

3 ☐ Tuscany/Lombard. *Like the Winchester Mystery House stairs: goes nowhere.*

■ **Portola.** A neighborhood showing strains.

3 ☐ Beeman Lane/Wabash & San Bruno.

3 ☐ Campbell/San Bruno & Bayshore.

3 ☐ Sunglow Lane/Gladstone & Silver.

■ **Pacific Heights.** A neighborhood that has maintained standards in architecture and appearance. Enviable views and private schools.

5 ☐ Baker/Vallejo & Broadway. *Plantings of Monterey pine, margueritas, hebe. Walk on the west side and experience stair walking vs. uphill walking!*

4 ☐ Broderick/Broadway & Vallejo. *One of the few stairways whose designer is known: Schubert & Friedman, 1979. View.*

3 ☐ Fillmore/Green & Vallejo. *Stop for extra breath on this sidewalk stairway, presented by the Fillmore Street Improvement Association in 1915.*

3 ☐ Gough/Clay, into Lafayette Park. *Near tennis courts.*

3 ☐ Gough/Washington, into Lafayette Park.

4 ☐ Green/Scott & Pierce. *Stairway imbedded in center of wide sidewalk.*

3 ☐ Laguna/Washington, into Lafayette Park. *Sunbathers in summer.*

5 ☐ Lyon/Green & Vallejo & Broadway. *Designed by Louis Upton, 1916. View. Complex arrangement of stairs, planting areas, landings.*

4 ☐ Normandie Terrace/Vallejo. *Built in 1938, not accepted by the city until 1976.*

3 ☐ Octavia/Washington & Jackson. *Surrounded by mansions. Stairways within island of cul-de-sac. Obviously planned, but for what? Decayed elegance.*

5 ☐ Pierce/Clay & Washington, into Alta Plaza. *Beautifully proportioned, extremely wide, tiered. Amid low shrubbery and lawn.*

3 ☐ Pierce/Jackson & Washington, into Alta Plaza. *Sunny. View to North Bay.*

3 ☐ Sacramento/Laguna & Gough, into Lafayette Park. *Stairway originally went to house of one Holladay, a squatter! Dog running area nearby.*

5 ☐ Scott/Clay & Washington, into Alta Plaza. *Elegant stairway surrounded by elaborate Victorians.*

5 ☐ Steiner/Clay & Washington, into Alta Plaza. *Beginning a series of off-cornered, off-centered, wide stairs.*

5 ☐ Steiner/Washington & Jackson, into Alta Plaza. *Imposing entrance to lunching bench and paths to four corners of the park.*

3 ☐ Vallejo/Scott & Pierce. *Sidewalk stairway.*

3 ☐ Webster/Broadway & Vallejo. *Sidewalk stairway across from Flood Mansion, which is now a private school.*

■ **Potrero Hill.** Beautiful weather and views—until developers can't be held off any longer.

3 ☐ Army/Evans & Mississippi.

3 ☐ Caroline/19th & 20th Streets. *Views of Bay Bridge and freeway network. Secluded.*

2 ☐ Mariposa/Utah & Potrero. *Sidewalk stairway.*

* Missouri/opposite No. 571 near Sierra, to Texas. *Two stairways going nowhere.*

3 ☐ Twenty-second Street/Arkansas & Wisconsin. *Rural. View.*

2 ☐ Twenty-second Street/Kansas & Rhode Island. *Sidewalk stairway. Very steep.*

4 ☐ Vermont/20th to 22nd Street. *Curly street. Several stairways radiating from successive cul-de-sacs. Stairway to McKinley Square. Great view.*

■ **Presidio.** Founded in 1776 by the Spanish; Moraga and Anza, leaders.

3 ☐ Barnard/Hicks, up to Presidio Blvd. *Exploring area.*

2 ☐ Presidio Boulevard/MacArthur Avenue & Letterman Boulevard. *Series of small stairways.*

■ **Richmond.** Known as the Sand Waste area in early days of San Francisco.

5 ☐ California/32nd Avenue & golf course, to Lincoln Park. *Surrounded by cypresses. Twenty-nine-foot-wide stairway with landings, benches. Footpath around to the Legion of Honor.*

1 ☐ El Camino del Mar/Palace of the Legion of Honor. *Come here*

for the setting, it's unsurpassed. It's criminal that the railing is so starkly ugly. Lots of paths to explore in this national urban park.

1 ☐ Forty-eighth Avenue/Balboa & Sutro Heights. *Magnificent view of wild ocean; take stairs on right-hand side. In front of 680 48th, well-worn footpath up to Sutro Heights.*

4 ☐ Lake/El Camino del Mar to 30th Avenue. *Stairways between three levels of Lake. Very pretty.*

4 ☐ Seacliff/from No. 330 toward China Beach. *In the elegant Seacliff neighborhood.*

4 ☐ Twenty-seventh Avenue/Seacliff & El Camino del Mar. *Beautiful area. Four brick stairways.*

2 ☐ Wood/Dicha & Lupine. *Used regularly by residents with their full grocery carts.*

■ **Russian Hill.** Graves of Russians buried on the hill account for the neighborhood name.

2 ☐ Broadway/Himmelman & Salmon Alley. Utilitarian.

5 ☐ Broadway/Jones & Taylor. *Very narrow, centered sidewalk stairway.*

5 ☐ Chestnut/Polk & Larkin. *In center of Chestnut cul-de-sac. Very wide. Foliage. Double staircase up to Larkin.*

3 ☐ Culebra Terrace/1256 Lombard & Chestnut. *Charming. Miniature 'village' islet. Terraced.*

5 ☐ Filbert/Hyde & Leavenworth. *Sidewalk stairway. Coit Tower straight ahead. 124 steps: a strenuous walk up a 31.5-percent grade.*

3 ☐ Florence/Broadway & Vallejo. *Charming. Pueblo Revival houses nearby. 1939 stairway.*

5 ☐ Upper Francisco/Upper Leavenworth & Hyde. *Ivy cascading down walls, urns, view to the north, pines.*

4 ☐ Green/Jones & Taylor. *Next to 940 Green, high-rise almost smack in front.*

5 ☐ Greenwich/Hyde & Larkin. *Set into tennis courts.*

5 ☐ Greenwich/Hyde & Leavenworth. *View.*

5 ☐ Havens/Leavenworth & Hyde. *Cul-de-sac: entrance only on west side of Leavenworth. Charming.*

1 ☐ Houston/Jones & Columbus. *Next to 2430 Jones.*

3 ☐ Hyde and Francisco. *Deeply grooved staired corner. Necessary.*

5 ☐ Jones/Filbert & Union & Green. *Nicely proportioned. Raised sidewalk stairway. Hard work. Stairs have a visual pattern of horizontal louvered shades.*

4 ☐ Larkin/Bay & Francisco. *Long series of stairs. Pass by reservoir paths.*

3 ☐ Larkin/Chestnut & Francisco to Bay. *Begins at 2745 Larkin. View of reservoir and slope of wild plants.*

4 ☐ Leavenworth/Chestnut & Francisco. *Walk on west side to long rampart, try both upper and lower approach.*

5 ☐ Lombard/Hyde & Leavenworth. *Curly here, straight there.*

2/5 ☐ Macondray Lane/Leavenworth & Jones, Union & Green. *The eastern section of Macondray is Shangri-la, the western is not.*

3 ☐ Montclair Terrace/Lombard & Chestnut. *Hidden.*

5 ☐ Vallejo/Jones & Taylor. *Retaining wall dates 1914. View. Entrance to special section of Vallejo, and houses designed by Willis Polk on Russian Hill Place. Stairways also designed by Polk.*

5 ☐ Vallejo/Mason & Taylor. *Winding.*

■ **South of Market.** Once an early residential neighborhood; now industrial.

3 ☐ Beale/Main & Fremont to Harrison. *Ed. Beale was the first to bring gold samples to the east coast, 1848. On old Rincon Hill, anchor of the Bay Bridge.*

* Lansing/First Street & Essex. *Freeway fumes with every breath: once (in Gold Rush times) this was an elegant neighborhood.*

■ **St. Francis Wood.** Architect-designed gates and fountains at boulevard entrance.

3 ☐ Junipero Serra/19th Avenue.

3 ☐ Portola/Claremont.

3 ☐ Portola/Santa Clara.

1 ☐ Stonestown Stairway/19th Avenue & Stonestown Center. *Across from Mercy High School.*

■ **Telegraph Hill.** Early photos show stairways literally hanging over the cliffs of this history-ridden neighborhood.

2 ☐ Bartol Alley/at 379 Broadway, to Montgomery & Prescott. *Franciscan formation under an adjacent house.*

4 ☐ Calhoun/upper to lower, Union & Montgomery. *View. Unexpected eye-opener.*

3 ☐ Child/Lombard & Telegraph Place. *Almost unseen. Form and function in accord.*

5 □ Filbert/Grant & Kearny. *Next to Garfield School. Steps of perfect proportion.*

3 □ Filbert/Kearny.

5 □ Filbert/Telegraph Hill Boulevard, Montgomery & Sansome. *Special, personalized stairway. Wonderful, extensive plantings.*

4 □ Francisco/Kearny & Grant. *An attractive access to Coit Tower.*

2 □ Genoa Place/Union, Kearny & Varennes.

4 □ Greenwich/Grant & Kearny. *An attractive way up to the summit of the hill and Coit Tower.*

5 □ Greenwich/Telegraph Boulevard & Montgomery & Sansome. *Moving a grand piano to a house on the Greenwich Stairs would be difficult.*

3 □ Julius Street/Lombard & Whiting. *Not easily seen.*

2 □ Kearny/Chestnut. *Wooden stairs.*

5 □ Kearny/Lombard & Telegraph Hill Boulevard. *View.*

4 □ Kearny/Vallejo & Broadway. *Total pedestrian block. Strenuous. Adjacent post-1906 houses are unfortunately disappearing.*

5 □ Lombard/Kearny & Telegraph Hill Boulevard. *View.*

4 □ Montgomery/Green & Union.

3 □ Montgomery/Union & Greenwich.

3 □ Pardee Alley/near Grant to Greenwich.

2 □ San Antonio Place/Vallejo to Kearny & Grant.

4 □ Union/Calhoun & east cliff of Telegraph Hill. *Closeup of geologic formation of the hill. View.*

3 □ Vallejo/Kearny & Montgomery.

■ **Twin Peaks.** A focal point for the entire city as outlined in the 1905 Burnham Beautification report, forgotten in the mad rush to rebuild after the 1906 earthquake and fire.

2 □ Burnett/opposite No. 535, upper to lower.

4 □ Clayton/Corbett. *View. Lovely transitional stairway. Fine specimen of a corner-rounding design.*

3 □ Clayton/Market. *Graceful corner-rounder.*

3 □ Copper/Greystone & Corbett, next to 301 Greystone & 592 Corbett. *Extraordinary view. Stairway in the process of disappearing.*

2 □ Crestline/at No. 70, to Parkridge. *View.*

2 □ Cuesta Court to Corbett.

4 □ Cuesta Court/Portola & Corbett. *Exceptional view. Cotoneaster and Monterey pines.*

4 □ Dixie/Burnett & Corbett. *Rural.*

3 □ Farnsworth/Edgewood & Willard. *Beautiful but shy.*

2 □ Fredela Lane/Clairview Court & Fairview Court.

2 □ Fredela Lane/Lower Marview & Clairview Court.

2 □ Gardenside/Burnett. *View.*

2 □ Gardenside/Parkridge. *Glorious views.*

5 □ Pemberton Place/Crown & Clayton. *View. Shangri-la, 1942-vintage stairway.*

■ **Upper Market.** The life cycle of this neighborhood is at a stable renaissance in its acceptance of its large gay population and quality of business enterprises.

2 □ Church/Market, down into MUNI Metro station. *Terrazzo stairway, ceramic tile walls.*

2 □ Clifford Terrace/Roosevelt. *Curving the corner.*

4 □ Corbett/at No. 336. *Behind No. 336 is a long alley and stairway.*

1 □ Corbett/17th Street. *The two steps serve the purpose of curving the corner.*

3 □ Corbin Place/17th Street & Corbett.

3 □ Danvers/18th Street & Market. *A 1946 stairway.*

3 □ Douglass/States & 17th Street. *Charming, tree-lined cul-de-sac with an assortment of Victorians.*

2 □ Glendale/Corbett.

3 □ Grand View/next to No. 600 Market. *View. Accompaniment to modified skywalk. Well-planted area.*

4 □ Henry/473 Roosevelt & Castro. *Cul-de-sac. Hidden. A charmer.*

5 □ Iron Alley/495 Corbett to 1499 Clayton and extension to Market. *View. Unusual sight from below. Wooden stairs. If you don't suffer from agoraphobia, walk down from Corbett and experience city elevations.*

3 □ Levant/States & Roosevelt. *High retaining wall covered with vines. Butterflies and chickadees abound in the foliage. Curved street complements stairs.*

3 □ Lower Terrace/Saturn. *Four short stairways that connect with Saturn/Ord stairway.*

2 □ Market/Grand View. *Hidden. Watch out for tree trunks.*

4 □ Market/Short.

4 □ Mono/Eagle & Market. *Part of a long twitton.*

3 ☐ Monument Way/Mt. Olympus. *View. You're at the geographical center of San Francisco.*

4 ☐ Monument Way/Upper Terrace. *View. Neighborly.*

1 ☐ Ord Court/at No. 2 to Douglass cul-de-sac. *Surprise.*

3 ☐ Ord Street/Storrie & Market down to Ord & 18th Street. *Happy muraled wall on 176 Ord at end of stairway.*

2 ☐ Roosevelt/17th Street. *Rounding a corner.*

3 ☐ Roosevelt Way/Lower Terrace. *Cotoneaster shrubs alongside.*

3 ☐ Saturn/Ord & 17th Street. *A lesser planetary stairway. No caring neighbors around.*

2 ☐ Saturn/Temple & 100 block Saturn. *Three series of four to five steps down to street. Good use of stair idea.*

3 ☐ Seventeenth Street/Clayton & Roosevelt to Upper Terrace. *Alongside large apartment buildings. Goes to a concentric circle where the view is fabulous.*

2 ☐ Seventeenth Street/Corbett. *Rounding the corner.*

2 ☐ Seventeenth Street/Mars. *Rounding a corner.*

2 ☐ Seventeenth Street/Roosevelt. *Rounding a corner.*

3 ☐ Stanton/Grand View & Market. *Hidden. Will soon be an archaeological find.*

4 ☐ Temple/Corbett & 17th Street. *Next to 4399 17th. Tiered plantings on both sides of stairs.*

5 ☐ Vulcan/Levant & Ord. *Not to be missed. Best of the planetaries. Most caring neighbors. Cobblestone terracing.*

■ **Western Addition.** This neighborhood survived the 1906 earthquake and grew and grew until it reached its peak during World War II.

* Arbol Lane/Turk & Anza Vista. *A street stairway.*

* Fulton/Steiner, into Alamo Square.

* Grove/Scott & Steiner, into Alamo Square.

* Hayes/Scott & Pierce. *Divided street, several stairways.*

* Pierce/Fulton, into Alamo Square.

* Sonora Lane/O'Farrell & Terra Vista.

* Steiner/Grove & Hayes, into Alamo Square.